Short Christmas Stories for Kids

25 Magical Tales for Your Christmas Countdown

Cozy Nook Books

Table of Contents

Introduction

Welcome, little listeners, to a world of wonder and delight! Are you ready for a magical Christmas journey tonight? Oh, the adventures we'll have together! We'll journey to the North Pole and peek into Santa's workshop. We'll soar through the night sky with reindeer and help elves solve tricky problems. We'll meet snowmen with warm hearts and gingerbread people with even warmer spirits.

But that's not all! We'll also explore what Christmas means right in your own neighborhood. We'll discover the joy of giving, the power of kindness, and the magic that happens when people come together to help one another.

And here's a little secret: in each story, there's a special message or lesson. It might be about friendship, courage, or the importance of believing in yourself. As you listen, see if you can spot these hidden treasures!

Now, I have a question for you: Have you ever wondered what it would be like to be a Christmas tree? Or perhaps you've thought about what toys do when no one is watching? Well, get ready, because we're going to explore all of these ideas and more!

As we read these stories together, I'll need your help. Sometimes, I might ask you questions or invite you to guess what happens next. Don't be shy – let your imagination soar! After all, your ideas and thoughts are what make these stories truly magical.

And remember, while Christmas comes but once a year, the spirit of the season – the love, the kindness, the joy of giving – is something you can carry with you always. These stories are here to remind you of that, to spark your imagination, and to fill your heart with the warmth of the holiday season.

So, are you ready to begin? Find a cozy spot, snuggle up with your favorite blanket or stuffed animal, and let's set off on our Christmas adventure together.

With each story, we'll paint a picture in your mind of snowy landscapes, twinkling stars, and the rosy cheeks of merry children. We'll fill your ears with the jingle of sleigh bells, the laughter of elves, and the gentle whoosh of snowflakes falling. And most importantly, we'll fill your heart with the true spirit of Christmas.

So, which story shall we start with? The choice is yours! Will it be a tale of a brave little reindeer? Or perhaps the story of a Christmas cookie that came to life? Wherever we begin, I promise you an unforgettable journey through the magic of Christmas.

Are you cozy? Are you ready? Then let's turn the page and step into a world of holiday wonder!

Chapter 1:
The Littlest Reindeer's Big Night

In a cozy barn at the very top of the world, where the Northern Lights dance across the sky in ribbons of green and purple, lived a tiny reindeer named Tinsel.

Can you guess why she was called Tinsel?

That's right! Her fur sparkled just like the shiny decorations on a Christmas tree. When the sunlight hit her coat, it looked as if she was covered in twinkling stars.

Tinsel was the smallest reindeer at the North Pole. Her antlers were no bigger than twigs, and her hooves were barely the size of bottle caps. The other reindeer towered over her like tall pine trees.

Every morning, Tinsel woke up early, eager to help with the Christmas preparations. She'd bounce out of her hay bed, shaking off snowflakes that had drifted in through the barn window overnight.

"Good morning, everyone!" Tinsel would chirp cheerfully. "What can I do to help today?"

The older reindeer would exchange glances and shake their heads. "Oh, Tinsel," they'd say, their voices a mixture of amusement and pity. "You're too small to pull the sleigh. You're too tiny to carry presents. Why don't you just watch the others work?"

But Tinsel had a big dream. She wanted to help Santa on Christmas Eve, just like the famous reindeer she admired so much. She'd spend hours watching Dasher, Dancer, Prancer, and Vixen practice their flying formations. Comet and Cupid would zoom overhead, while Donner and Blitzen worked on their landing techniques. And of course, there was

Rudolph, whose bright red nose lit up the night sky.

"One day," Tinsel would whisper to herself, "I'll fly with them. I just know it!"

Every day, rain or shine (or more accurately, snow or blizzard), Tinsel practiced flying. She leaped and bounded across the snowy fields, trying to stay in the air just a little bit longer each time.

"Whoosh! Look at me go!" she'd cry, as she zoomed around the barn. She'd jump from snowdrift to snowdrift, pretending each leap was taking her higher into the sky.

The other reindeer just laughed. "Silly Tinsel," they'd say, nudging each other with their antlers. "You'll never be big enough to join Santa's team. Why don't you help the elves wrap presents instead?"

But Tinsel didn't give up. "I'll show them," she thought, her determination growing stronger with each chuckle and pitying glance. "One day, I'll prove that even the littlest reindeer can do big things!"

As the days grew shorter and Christmas drew nearer, the North Pole buzzed with even more activity. Elves scurried about, putting finishing touches on toys and checking lists twice. The reindeer intensified their training, knowing the big night was almost upon them.

Tinsel tried to help wherever she could. She'd offer to taste-test the candy canes (a job she particularly enjoyed), or to squeeze into tight spots to retrieve dropped tools for the elves. But more often than not, she was gently shooed away.

"It's okay, Tinsel," Santa would say kindly, patting her on the head. "Your time will come. For now, why don't you go and play?"

But Tinsel didn't want to play. She wanted to be useful, to be part of the magic of Christmas. So, she kept practicing, kept trying, kept believing.

One chilly morning, just three days before Christmas, Tinsel had an idea. She noticed that some of the smaller presents were tricky for the larger reindeer to move without damaging the wrapping paper.

"I can help with those!" she exclaimed, carefully picking up a small, delicately wrapped box with her mouth.

Mrs. Claus, who was overseeing the gift sorting, smiled warmly. "Why, thank you, Tinsel! That's very thoughtful of you."

For the next two days, Tinsel worked tirelessly, moving small gifts from the workshop to the sorting area. She may not have been able to carry the big presents, but she could handle lots of little ones! The elves began to appreciate her help, and even some of the other reindeer nodded approvingly as they passed by.

Finally, it was Christmas Eve. The North Pole was a flurry of last-minute activity. Elves dashed to and from, loading the last presents onto Santa's sleigh. The reindeer were getting into position, pawing at the ground eagerly, ready for their big night.

Tinsel watched from the sidelines, her heart swelling with excitement even though she knew she wouldn't be joining them. "Maybe next year," she thought, trying to stay positive.

But wait! What was that sound?

"Achoo!" It was Rudolph! His nose wasn't glowing red – it was running! Poor Rudolph had caught a terrible cold.

"Oh, Rudolph," Santa said, his brow furrowed with concern. "You can't fly like this. You need to rest and get better."

Rudolph sniffled miserably. "But Santa," he protested weakly, "without my nose, how will you find your way through Crooked Canyon? It's too narrow and dark for the other reindeer to see!"

A hush fell over the gathered elves and reindeer. Crooked Canyon was a notoriously tricky part of the route, with tight turns and low-hanging icicles. Without Rudolph's bright nose to light the way, it would be nearly impossible to navigate safely.

"Oh no!" cried Santa, his usual jolly demeanor replaced with worry. "Without Rudolph's bright nose, we might not be able to deliver presents to all the children! What are we going to do?"

All the big reindeer looked at each other, their earlier confidence fading. They shuffled their hooves nervously, each one hoping someone else would have a solution.

Suddenly, a small voice piped up. "I can do it, Santa!"

It was Tinsel! She had been listening from nearby and saw her chance to help.

The other reindeer couldn't believe their ears. "You?" they laughed, some of them a bit unkindly. "But you're so small! You've never even flown with the team before!"

Tinsel felt her cheeks grow hot with embarrassment, but she stood her ground. "I may be small," she said, her voice growing stronger, "but that's exactly why I can help! I can fit through the tightest spaces in Crooked Canyon. I've been practicing my flying every day. Please, Santa, let me try!"

Santa looked thoughtful. He stroked his white beard and said, "Hmm... maybe that's exactly what we need. Sometimes the biggest problems need the smallest solutions."

He turned to the other reindeer. "What do you think, team? Shall we give Tinsel a chance?"

The reindeer huddled together, whispering among themselves. Finally, Dasher stepped forward. "We're willing if you are, Santa," he said. "Tinsel has been working hard, and we've all seen how helpful she's been with the small packages. Maybe her size really is an advantage this time."

Santa's eyes twinkled as he turned back to Tinsel. "Well, little one, are you ready for a big adventure?"

Tinsel's heart felt like it might burst with joy. "Oh, yes, Santa! I'm ready! I won't let you down, I promise!"

Before she knew it, Tinsel found herself at the front of the team, right next to Dasher. Her little heart was pounding with a mixture of excitement and nervousness. This was her big chance, the moment she'd been dreaming of!

"Now, Tinsel," Santa said gently, "your job is very important. When we reach Crooked Canyon, you'll need to guide the team through. Your eyes are younger and sharper, and your small size will help you spot paths the others might miss. Can you do that?"

Tinsel nodded solemnly. "I can do it, Santa. I'll do my very best!"

"Ho ho ho!" Santa's laugh boomed out. "Then let's be off! On Dasher, on Dancer, on Prancer and Vixen! On Comet, on Cupid, on Donner and Blitzen! And leading the way, our littlest reindeer, Tinsel!"

And they were off! Up, up into the starry sky they flew. Tinsel felt the cold wind rushing through her fur, and for a moment, she felt a flicker of doubt. What if she couldn't do it? What if she let everyone down?

But then she remembered all her practice, all her determination. She could do this. She had to!

Soon, they reached Crooked Canyon. It was so dark and narrow, the big reindeer had to squint to see. Icicles hung down like crystal daggers, and the canyon walls twisted and turned unpredictably.

But not Tinsel! Her small size was perfect for the twisting path. She zipped left and right, her eyes darting everywhere, taking in every detail.

"Duck, everyone!" she called as they passed under a low icicle. "Now, turn right! Great job! Watch out for that outcropping on the left!"

The other reindeer followed her instructions perfectly, trusting in her guidance. Santa held on tight to the reins, a proud smile on his face.

As they neared the end of the canyon, Tinsel spotted a particularly tricky turn. "Everyone, we need to bank hard to the left, then immediately right!" she called out. "It's going to be tight, but we can make it!"

The team responded as one, executing the maneuver flawlessly. As they emerged from the canyon into the open night sky, a cheer went up from all the reindeer.

"We did it!" Dasher exclaimed. "And it's all thanks to you, Tinsel!"

Tinsel felt a warmth spreading through her chest that had nothing to do with flying. She had done it! She had proven that even the littlest reindeer could make a big difference.

Thanks to Tinsel's guidance, Santa delivered every present to every child in that town, right on time. As they flew away, Santa reached forward and patted Tinsel's head. "Well done, little one," he said, his voice full of pride. "You've saved Christmas for all those boys and girls. Your size wasn't a weakness at all – it was your greatest strength!"

Tinsel's heart swelled with joy and pride. She had done it! She had achieved her dream and helped Santa on Christmas Eve.

From that day on, no one at the North Pole ever underestimated Tinsel again. The other reindeer apologized for doubting her, and she was welcomed as a full member of the team. They all learned that sometimes, the biggest heroes come in the smallest packages.

And Tinsel? Well, she just kept on dreaming big and trying her best, because she knew now that anything is possible if you believe in yourself.

So, little ones, remember Tinsel's story. No matter how small you might feel, you have special gifts that can help others. You just have to believe in yourself and never give up!

The next time you see a Christmas tree sparkling with tinsel, think of the littlest reindeer who made the biggest difference. And remember, just like those shiny strands make the tree more beautiful, your unique qualities make the world a brighter place.

Chapter 2:
The Christmas Cookie Mix-Up

In Santa's workshop at the North Pole, where the air always smelled of peppermint and pine, there lived an elf named Jingle. Now, Jingle wasn't like the other elves. Where they were graceful, he was clumsy. Where they were organized, he was... well, let's just say his workspace looked like it had been hit by a tinsel tornado.

But do you know what made Jingle special? He had the biggest heart of any elf in the North Pole!

One chilly December morning, just a week before Christmas, Santa made an announcement that sent excited whispers through the workshop.

"My dear elves," Santa's jolly voice boomed, "it's time for our annual Christmas cookie baking competition!"

The elves cheered, their pointy ears wiggling with excitement. You see, every year, the elves compete to bake the most delicious Christmas cookies. The winner got the honor of having their cookies served to Santa on Christmas Eve.

"This year," Santa continued, his eyes twinkling, "I'm looking for something extra special. Something magical!"

Jingle's heart leapt. This was his chance to show everyone what he could do! He might not be the best at making toys, but he loved to bake. "I'm going to win this year," he thought determinedly. "I'll make the most magical cookies Santa has ever tasted!"

As the other elves rushed off to gather their ingredients, Jingle skipped to the workshop kitchen, humming a merry tune. He pulled out bowls and spoons, sugar and butter, and reached for the flour...

Oh no! In his excitement, Jingle had knocked over a shelf! Bags of flour, sugar, and a mysterious sparkling powder tumbled to the floor, spilling everywhere.

"Oops," Jingle muttered, his cheeks turning as red as Santa's coat. He quickly scooped up what he could, filling his flour bag with the white powder on the floor. In his haste, he didn't notice that some of the sparkling powder had mixed in too.

Can you guess what that sparkling powder was? That's right - magic dust!

Unaware of his mistake, Jingle began to bake. He mixed and stirred, rolled and cut, humming all the while. Soon, the kitchen was filled with the delicious aroma of baking cookies.

"They're ready!" Jingle exclaimed as he pulled the cookies from the oven. They looked perfect - golden brown and shaped like stars and Christmas trees.

But as Jingle reached out to take a cookie, something very strange happened. The cookie... floated away!

"What in the jingle bells?" Jingle gasped.

One by one, the cookies began to rise off the baking sheet. They floated up, up, up, until they were bobbing near the ceiling like edible balloons.

Jingle's eyes grew wide as flying saucers. "Oh no," he whispered. "What have I done?"

Just then, Twinkle, another elf, poked her head into the kitchen. "Hey Jingle, how's the baking -- GREAT CANDY CANES!" she exclaimed, her jaw dropping at the sight of the floating cookies.

"Twinkle!" Jingle cried. "Help! My cookies are flying away!"

Twinkle rushed into the kitchen, trying to grab the cookies. But they dodged her grasp, zooming around like sugary shooting stars.

"We need to catch them before they escape!" Twinkle shouted.

But it was too late. The cookies had found the kitchen door. They soared out into the workshop, leaving a trail of sparkling sugar behind them.

"Oh no, oh no, oh no!" Jingle wailed. "Quick, we have to catch them before Santa sees!"

Jingle and Twinkle raced after the runaway cookies. But catching them was harder than trying to pin down a cloud. The cookies zipped and zagged, loop-de-looped and zig-zagged through the workshop.

Chaos erupted in the workshop. Elves dove for cover as cookies whizzed past their pointed ears. Toys toppled from shelves as the flying treats zoomed by.

"Duck!" shouted an elf as a gingerbread man soared overhead.

"Watch out!" yelled another as a sugar cookie nearly collided with a stack of teddy bears.

Jingle and Twinkle chased the cookies, armed with nets usually used for catching runaway toy airplanes. But the cookies were too quick, always staying just out of reach.

"We need... more help," Jingle gasped, out of breath from the chase.

Twinkle nodded, then cupped her hands around her mouth. "COOKIE EMERGENCY!" she shouted at the top of her lungs.

Instantly, every elf in the workshop stopped what they were doing. In the North Pole, a cookie emergency was serious business indeed!

"The cookies are flying!" Jingle explained quickly. "We need to catch them before they escape the workshop!"

The elves sprang into action. They grabbed nets, opened empty toy sacks, and formed a giant elf pyramid to reach the higher-flying cookies. But those tricky treats were determined to stay free.

Suddenly, the workshop doors burst open. In walked Santa, followed by his team of reindeer who were there for a routine checkup.

"Ho ho ho! What's all this commotion about?" Santa asked, brushing snow from his beard.

Then he looked up. His eyes grew as round as Christmas ornaments at the sight of cookies zooming around the workshop like edible comets.

"My goodness!" Santa exclaimed. "I've seen a lot of things in my time, but flying cookies? That's a new one!"

Jingle stepped forward, his pointy shoes shuffling nervously. "It's my fault, Santa," he admitted, his voice quivering. "I was trying to make magical cookies for the competition, but I think I accidentally used magic dust instead of flour."

He hung his head, waiting to be scolded. But instead, he heard a familiar chuckle.

"Ho ho ho!" Santa's laugh filled the workshop. "Well, Jingle, you certainly succeeded in making magical cookies!"

Jingle looked up, hardly daring to believe his pointy ears. "You... you're not mad?"

Santa's eyes twinkled. "Mad? My dear Jingle, this is exactly the kind of magic I was hoping for! Although," he added with a wink, "perhaps a bit more... airborne than I expected."

Just then, Dasher, one of the reindeer, spoke up. "Um, Santa? I think I might be able to help catch these cookies."

Santa nodded. "Good thinking, Dasher! Reindeer, to the sky!"

The reindeer leaped into action, soaring gracefully around the workshop. With their speed and agility, they were much better equipped to chase the flying cookies than the elves.

Dasher and Dancer zigzagged through the air, corralling cookies with their antlers. Prancer and Vixen worked as a team, herding the treats towards Comet and Cupid, who caught them in mid-air. Donner and Blitzen swooped and swerved, snatching cookies left and right.

"Look at them go!" Jingle cheered, his earlier worries forgotten in the excitement of the chase.

The elves watched in awe as the reindeer performed an aerial ballet, slowly but surely catching every last cookie. Finally, Rudolph swooped down with the last cookie, a twinkling sugar star, perched on his red nose.

"Well done, everyone!" Santa boomed, clapping his hands. "Now, let's see about these magical cookies."

Cautiously, Santa picked up a cookie. It quivered in his hand but didn't fly away. He took a bite, and his face lit up like a Christmas tree.

"Delicious!" he declared. "Light as air and twice as tasty. Jingle, my boy, I think you've won this year's competition!"

Jingle could hardly believe his ears. "Really, Santa? Even after all the trouble I caused?"

Santa placed a gentle hand on Jingle's shoulder. "Jingle, sometimes the best magic happens by accident. These cookies are perfect! They're light enough to float, which means they won't weigh down my sleigh. And they're small enough to eat quickly during my Christmas Eve journey. You've created the perfect mid-flight snack!"

Jingle's heart swelled with pride. His mistake had turned into something wonderful after all!

From that day on, Jingle was in charge of baking the special flying cookies for Santa's Christmas Eve journey. The other elves even asked him to teach them his secret recipe (though they were careful to use just a pinch of magic dust).

And every Christmas Eve, as Santa soared through the night sky delivering presents, he would reach into his pocket and pull out one of Jingle's special cookies. As he munched on the floating treat, he would think fondly of the clumsy but well-meaning elf who had created such a marvelous mistake.

So, little ones, remember Jingle's story. Sometimes, what seems like a big mistake can turn into something magical. The next time you bite into a Christmas cookie, who knows? It might just try to float away!

Chapter 3:
Jingle the Elf's Silent Night Adventure

In Santa's workshop, where laughter echoed and toy hammers tapped, there lived an elf named Jingle. Now, Jingle wasn't called Jingle because he liked to sing (though he did). He got his name from the tiny silver bell he always wore on the tip of his hat.

Can you imagine the sound it made? Jingle-jingle-jingle with every step!

All the other elves could always tell when Jingle was coming. "Here comes Jingle!" they'd say with a smile as they heard his bell approaching. Some elves found the constant jingling a bit much, but most agreed it added to the festive atmosphere of the workshop.

Jingle loved his bell. It had been a gift from Santa himself on Jingle's first day as an official North Pole elf. "This bell," Santa had said, his eyes twinkling, "is very special. It will help you spread Christmas cheer wherever you go."

And spread cheer he did! Jingle's bell became famous throughout the workshop. When toy-making got tough and elves got grumpy, Jingle would dance by, his bell tinkling merrily, and soon everyone would be smiling again.

But Jingle's bell wasn't just for fun. Oh no! It was very important. You see, on Christmas Eve, Jingle had a special job. He was in charge of the "Sound Check Team."

What's a Sound Check Team, you ask? Well, let me tell you!

On Christmas Eve, when Santa delivers presents, it's very important that he doesn't wake up the children. So Jingle and his team would go into each house first, testing how noisy or quiet things were. Jingle would jingle his bell, and if it was too loud, they knew Santa had to be extra careful.

As this Christmas Eve approached, Jingle was more excited than ever. He polished his bell until it shone like a star and practiced his quietest tiptoes. He even gave seminars to the other elves on "The Art of Silent Gift-Giving."

"Remember, everyone, soft hands make silent nights!"

The other elves would giggle at Jingle's serious expression, but they had to admit, he was the best at being quiet when it counted.

"This year," Jingle thought, "I'll be the quietest, most helpful elf ever!"

Finally, the big night arrived. The workshop was buzzing with activity as the elves loaded Santa's sleigh with presents. Jingle watched the clock, waiting for his turn to join Santa on his journey.

He triple-checked his "Silent Night" kit: soft-soled shoes, oil for squeaky doors, and a pair of fluffy earmuffs (in case he needed to muffle his own bell in extremely quiet houses).

At last, the time came. Jingle rushed to the sleigh, his bell jingling merrily. But in his excitement, he didn't notice a low-hanging candy cane...

"Ouch!" Jingle rubbed his head where he'd bumped it. But wait... something didn't sound right. Where was the familiar jingle?

Jingle reached up to touch his hat, and his heart sank. His bell was gone!

"Oh no! My bell! Where is it?"

Jingle looked around frantically, but the workshop was so busy, and there were so many shiny things, he couldn't spot his little silver bell anywhere.

He dropped to his hands and knees, crawling around and peering under workbenches and gift-wrapping stations. Other elves gave him curious looks.

"Jingle? What are you doing down there?" asked Tinsel, a gift-wrapping expert.

"My bell!" Jingle whispered urgently. "I've lost my bell! I can't do the Sound Check without it!"

Tinsel's eyes widened. "Oh no! Don't worry, we'll help you find it!"

Soon, a small army of elves was searching for Jingle's bell. They looked in toy boxes and cookie jars, under Christmas trees and behind snowmen decorations. But the bell was nowhere to be found.

"Jingle!" Santa called. "It's time to go! Are you ready?"

Jingle's pointy ears drooped. How could he do his job without his bell? But he couldn't let Santa down. Taking a deep breath, he climbed into the sleigh.

"I'm ready, Santa," he said, trying to sound braver than he felt.

Santa looked at him curiously. "Jingle, where's your bell?"

Jingle's lower lip trembled. "I... I lost it, Santa. I'm so sorry! I don't know how I'll do the Sound Check without it!"

Santa's eyes twinkled kindly. "Jingle, my boy, do you think the bell is what makes you good at your job?"

Jingle blinked in surprise. "Well... isn't it?"

Santa chuckled softly. "The bell is a tool, Jingle. But the real skill? That comes from in here." He tapped Jingle gently on the chest. "You have the quietest hands and the lightest step of any elf I know. Bell or no bell, I know you'll do a wonderful job tonight."

Jingle felt a warmth spread through him at Santa's words. Maybe Santa was right. Maybe he could do this, even without his bell.

And with a whoosh and a sprinkle of magic dust, they were off into the starry night sky.

As they approached the first house, Jingle began to worry again. How would he test the noise without his bell?

"Alright, Jingle," Santa whispered. "Time for the sound check!"

Jingle gulped and nodded. He tiptoed into the house, his feet barely making a sound on the soft carpet. But how could he test the noise level?

Then, he had an idea. He picked up a small ornament from a nearby Christmas tree and gently tapped it against a table.

The sound was barely audible. Jingle smiled and gave Santa a thumbs up. They could proceed!

At the next house, Jingle faced a new challenge. The floor was made of creaky wooden boards!

Jingle froze. This was too noisy! But then he remembered something he'd learned in elf acrobatics class. Very carefully, he did a series of cartwheels across the room, avoiding the creaky spots.

When he reached the Christmas tree, he turned and saw Santa watching him with an amused twinkle in his eye. Jingle grinned and gestured for Santa to follow his path.

As the night went on, Jingle found more and more creative ways to do his job without his bell. He used hand signals to communicate with Santa, tapped out quiet rhythms to test noise levels, and even used a feather he found to check for drafts that might make noise.

In one house, he encountered a curious cat that seemed determined to meow and wake everyone up. Thinking quickly, Jingle pulled a soft toy mouse from Santa's sack and used it to silently lead the cat into another room.

"Phew! That was close!"

In another home, he had to stop a dripping faucet that was making too much noise. Using his elf magic, he created a tiny ice cap for the faucet, silencing the drip until morning.

At one point, they visited a house where a little girl was still awake, trying to catch a glimpse of Santa. Jingle held his breath, worried they'd be spotted. But then he had an idea. He found a small music box and wound it up very gently. The soft, soothing lullaby drifted through the air, and soon the little girl's eyes began to droop.

Santa gave Jingle a silent thumbs up as they tiptoed past the now-sleeping child.

With each challenge, Jingle grew more confident. He realized that he didn't need his bell to be helpful. In fact, sometimes being silent made him even more effective!

As the night wore on, Jingle and Santa fell into a smooth, silent rhythm. Jingle would go ahead, using his creativity and quick thinking to ensure a quiet path. Santa would follow, placing presents under trees and filling stockings without making a sound.

It was like a beautiful, silent dance of Christmas magic.

In one house, they found a note from a child asking Santa how he stayed so quiet. Jingle smiled and quickly sketched a picture of himself doing a cartwheel, which Santa left next to the milk and cookies.

At another home, a dog started to stir as they entered. Jingle quickly fashioned a small dream catcher from some spare ribbon and hung it over the dog's bed. The pup immediately fell into a deep sleep, dreaming of chasing squirrels instead of barking at Santa.

As dawn approached, Jingle realized something amazing. Not only had they not woken anyone up, but they were actually ahead of schedule! His creative solutions had made their journey even more efficient than usual.

Finally, as the first light of dawn began to color the sky, Santa and Jingle returned to the North Pole. The other elves gathered around, eager to hear about their night.

"Ho ho ho!" Santa laughed (quietly, of course – some elves were sleeping after their long night of work). "Jingle, my boy, I must say, this was the quietest Christmas Eve journey we've ever had!"

Jingle beamed with pride. "Really, Santa?"

Santa nodded. "Indeed! Your creativity and quick thinking kept us quieter than ever. Why, I don't think we woke a single mouse, let alone a child!"

The other elves cheered (softly) and patted Jingle on the back. Jingle felt a warm glow of happiness inside. He had done it! Even without his bell, he had been the best helper he could be.

Just then, Twinkle, another elf, came running up. "Jingle! I found your bell! It was caught on a candy cane in the workshop."

She held out the tiny silver bell. Jingle looked at it, then at Santa, then back at the bell. Finally, he smiled and shook his head.

"Thank you, Twinkle," he said. "But I think I'll save the bell for special occasions from now on. I've learned that sometimes, the best help comes silently."

Santa's eyes twinkled with pride. "Well said, Jingle. You've learned an important lesson. Sometimes, we don't need bells and whistles to do a good job. Often, it's the quiet, thoughtful actions that make the biggest difference."

From that day on, Jingle became known as the quietest elf in Santa's workshop. But he was also known as one of the most creative and helpful. And every Christmas Eve, he would lead the Sound Check Team, using his ingenuity and silent skills to help Santa deliver presents without a sound.

He kept his bell, of course, hanging it on his bedpost where he could see it every night. It reminded him of an important lesson: true magic doesn't always announce itself with bells and whistles. Sometimes, it works best in silence.

So, little ones, the next time you wake up on Christmas morning to find presents under your tree, remember Jingle the elf. And know that sometimes, the most magical things happen in the quietest moments.

Chapter 4:
The Polar Bear Who Saved Christmas

In the frozen reaches of the Arctic, where the Northern Lights dance across the sky and the wind whispers secrets to the snow, there lived a polar bear named Frost. Frost wasn't like other polar bears. While they were content to hunt seals and fish, Frost had always been curious about the world beyond the ice.

Can you imagine a polar bear who dreamed of adventure?

Frost would often sit on the highest ice ridge, gazing at the stars and wondering what lay beyond the endless white horizon. The other polar bears thought he was a bit strange, but Frost didn't mind. He knew that somewhere out there, adventure was waiting.

Little did Frost know that his greatest adventure was about to begin, and it would start on a very special night - Christmas Eve.

As the sun dipped below the horizon, painting the sky in brilliant shades of pink and purple, Frost noticed something unusual. A streak of red flashed across the starry night, followed by the faint sound of jingling bells.

"What could that be?" Frost wondered aloud, his breath forming little clouds in the frigid air.

Suddenly, the red streak wobbled and began to descend rapidly. Frost's keen eyes widened as he realized it wasn't a shooting star, but some kind of flying vehicle!

With a thunderous crash that sent snow flying in all directions, the mysterious object landed not far from where Frost was standing. Without hesitation, the curious polar bear lumbered towards the crash site, his massive paws leaving deep imprints in the snow.

As Frost approached, he couldn't believe his eyes. There, half-buried in a snowdrift, was a large red sleigh. And struggling to free himself from a tangled mess of reins was none other than...

Can you guess who it was?

That's right! It was Santa Claus himself!

"Oh, dear me," Santa muttered, brushing snow from his red coat. "This is quite a pickle we've found ourselves in, isn't it, boys?"

The reindeer, looking a bit dazed from the crash, nodded in agreement.

Frost, overcome with excitement and concern, called out, "Hello there! Are you alright? Do you need help?"

Santa turned, startled by the deep, rumbling voice. His eyes widened at the sight of the enormous polar bear, but then he relaxed, seeing the gentle concern in Frost's eyes.

"Why, hello there, my large furry friend!" Santa said warmly. "I must say, I'm in a bit of a predicament. You see, my sleigh seems to have had a bit of an accident."

Frost padded closer, examining the sleigh. One of the runners was cracked, and several of the reins had snapped during the crash.

"Oh my," Frost said. "That doesn't look good at all. But maybe I can help! What's your name, sir?"

Santa chuckled, his belly shaking like a bowl full of jelly. "Ho ho ho! I'm Santa Claus, of course! And who might you be?"

"I'm Frost," the polar bear replied, puffing up with pride. "And I'd be honored to help you, Santa Claus!"

Santa's eyes twinkled. "Well, Frost, I'd be most grateful for your assistance. You see, it's Christmas Eve, and I have presents to deliver to all the children of the world. But with my sleigh damaged, I'm afraid Christmas might be in jeopardy!"

Frost's heart raced with excitement. This was his chance for a real adventure! "Don't worry, Santa," he said confidently. "We'll figure something out!"

First, they needed to repair the sleigh's runner. Frost had an idea. He lumbered off and returned with a long, sturdy piece of driftwood he'd found washed up on the shore months ago.

"Will this work?" he asked, presenting it to Santa.

Santa's eyes lit up. "Why, that's perfect, Frost! But how will we shape it to fit the sleigh?"

Frost grinned, revealing his impressive teeth. "Leave that to me!" With careful precision, he used his strong jaws to gnaw the wood into the perfect shape.

Next, they needed to mend the broken reins. Frost remembered the long strands of tough seaweed that grew in a nearby unfrozen patch of sea.

"I'll be right back!" he called, diving into the icy water.

When Frost resurfaced, he had several long strands of seaweed clenched gently between his teeth. Santa was amazed at how strong yet flexible they were - perfect for replacing the broken reins!

As they worked together to repair the sleigh, Santa regaled Frost with tales of his Christmas Eve journeys around the world. Frost listened in wonder, his eyes shining with excitement.

"Santa," Frost asked as they tied the last knot in the new reins, "what's it like, seeing all those different places in one night?"

Santa smiled kindly at the curious polar bear. "It's magical, Frost. Every home, every child, every corner of the world has its own special kind of beauty. But I must say, the Arctic has always been one of my favorite stops. The stark beauty of the ice and snow, the brave animals like yourself who call this harsh land home - it's truly breathtaking."

Frost felt a warm glow of pride for his Arctic home.

Finally, after what seemed like hours of work, the sleigh was repaired. Santa clapped his mittened hands together in delight.

"Wonderful job, Frost! You've saved Christmas!"

But as Santa prepared to take off, he noticed something wasn't quite right. Donner, one of his reindeer, was limping slightly from the crash.

"Oh dear," Santa fretted. "Donner's hurt his leg. He won't be able to fly like this, and without all nine reindeer, the sleigh won't have enough power to take off!"

Frost's heart sank. After all their hard work, would Christmas still be ruined? Then, an idea struck him.

"Santa," he said, straightening up to his full, impressive height, "what if I took Donner's place? I'm strong, and I've always dreamed of seeing the world beyond the Arctic. I promise I'll do my very best!"

Santa stroked his beard thoughtfully. "Well, I've never had a polar bear pull my sleigh before. But then again, I've never had a polar bear save Christmas before either! Frost, my dear friend, I would be honored to have you join my team for this special night."

And so, with Donner tucked safely in the sleigh and Frost harnessed in his place, Santa prepared for takeoff once more.

"Now, Frost," Santa explained, "to fly, you must believe. Believe in the magic of Christmas, believe in the joy you're bringing to children all over the world, and most importantly, believe in yourself!"

Frost closed his eyes, concentrating hard. He thought of all the children waiting for their presents, of the wonder and magic of Christmas that Santa had described. He thought of his own dream of adventure, finally coming true.

Suddenly, Frost felt his paws leave the ground! He opened his eyes in amazement to find himself soaring through the air, the Arctic landscape shrinking below him.

"Ho ho ho!" Santa laughed joyously. "Well done, Frost! Now, on Dasher, on Dancer, on Prancer and Vixen! On Comet, on Cupid, on Donner and Blitzen! And Frost, our Christmas hero! To all the children of the world!"

And off they flew into the night sky, the Northern Lights seeming to wave them on their way.

What an adventure Frost had that night! He soared over bustling cities and quiet villages, across vast oceans and towering mountains. He saw children of all kinds, in homes of all types, each one filled with the magic of Christmas.

As the night went on, Frost found he could fly as naturally as he could swim. He reveled in the feeling of the wind in his fur and the stars seeming close enough to touch.

Just as the first light of dawn began to color the eastern sky, Santa and his team returned to the Arctic to drop off Frost and pick up the now-recovered Donner.

"Frost, my friend," Santa said, his eyes twinkling with gratitude, "you have truly saved Christmas. Your quick thinking, your strength, and your belief in the magic of the season made all of this possible."

Frost felt a warmth in his heart that had nothing to do with his thick fur. "Thank you, Santa," he said. "This has been the greatest adventure of my life."

Santa reached into his sack and pulled out a small package wrapped in shimmering paper. "A little something to remember this night," he said, handing it to Frost.

As Santa's sleigh disappeared into the dawn sky, Frost carefully opened his gift. Inside was a beautiful snow globe. But this was no ordinary snow globe. Inside, he could see the whole world in miniature, and when he shook it, instead of snow, tiny stars swirled around, just like the ones he'd flown among.

From that day on, Frost had wonderful tales to tell the other polar bears. Some believed him, some didn't, but Frost didn't mind. He knew the truth of that magical Christmas Eve.

And every year on Christmas Eve, Frost would sit on his favorite ice ridge, watching the sky. And every year, he would see a streak of red flash by. If you listened very carefully, you might just hear a faint "Ho ho ho!" on the wind, and an answering rumble of polar bear laughter.

So, little ones, the next time you see a polar bear in a picture or at the zoo, remember Frost. Remember that great adventures and acts of kindness can come from the most unexpected places. And who knows? Maybe that polar bear is dreaming of flying with Santa too!

Chapter 5:
The Upside-Down Christmas Tree

c⟨∞⟩ɔ

In a cozy little house on Maple Street, lived the Johnson family. There was Dad with his jolly laugh, Mom with her warm smile, ten-year-old Emma with her bright ideas, and seven-year-old Max with his mischievous grin.

Every year, the Johnsons had a special tradition. On the first day of December, they'd all pile into their old station wagon and drive to Pete's Christmas Tree Farm to pick out the perfect tree.

"All right, troops! Operation Perfect Tree is a go! Everyone bundle up!"

This year was no different. The family sang carols as they drove, their breath fogging up the windows in the chilly air. When they arrived at Pete's, the scent of pine filled their noses, and their eyes sparkled with excitement.

"Remember," Mom said, her voice warm but firm, "we're looking for a tree that's just the right height for our living room. Not too tall, not too short."

Emma and Max nodded solemnly, but their eyes were already darting from tree to tree, each one more magnificent than the last.

After an hour of "How about this one?" and "No, too bushy" and "Wait, I think I see the perfect one over there!", they finally found it. A beautiful Fraser fir, just the right height and fullness.

With the tree secured to the roof of their car, the Johnsons headed home, ready to begin decorating. But as Dad and Mom struggled to bring the tree inside, disaster struck.

The tree slipped from their grasp and fell to the floor with a heavy thud.

"Oh no!" Max cried, his eyes wide.

Emma rushed over to inspect the damage. The fall had bent several branches, and a good portion of the needles now lay scattered on the floor.

"Well, that's... not ideal."

Dad scratched his head, looking at the sad state of their once-perfect tree. "Maybe we can prop it up in the corner? The bent side can face the wall."

But as they tried to stand the tree up, they encountered a new problem. The fall had damaged the trunk, and now the tree wouldn't stay straight in the stand. It kept leaning to one side, threatening to topple over again.

The family stood around the fallen tree, their earlier excitement deflated like a punctured balloon. Max's lower lip began to tremble, and even Dad's usual jolly smile had faded.

But then, Emma's eyes lit up with an idea.

"Wait! I know what we can do!"

Everyone turned to look at her, curious.

"What if," Emma said slowly, her idea taking shape as she spoke, "we hang the tree from the ceiling? Upside down!"

For a moment, there was silence. Then Max burst into giggles.

"An upside-down Christmas tree? That's silly!"

Mom and Dad exchanged glances, unsure.

"I don't know, sweetie. That sounds... unusual."

But Emma wasn't giving up. "Think about it! The bent branches won't matter if it's upside down. And we won't have to worry about it falling over again. Plus," she added with a grin, "it'll be the most unique Christmas tree in the whole neighborhood!"

The more they thought about it, the more intrigued they became. Dad's eyes twinkled with the challenge of figuring out how to hang a tree from the ceiling. Mom started to smile, imagining how they could decorate it.

"You know, in some European countries, they used to hang trees upside down. It's actually an old tradition!"

Max was practically bouncing with excitement now. "Can we do it? Please, please, please?"

Dad laughed, his jolly spirit returning. "Well, why not? Let's give it a try!"

What followed was an afternoon of problem-solving, teamwork, and more than a few laughs. Dad dug out his toolbox and, with Emma's help, figured out a way to securely fasten the tree's trunk to a hook in the ceiling.

Mom and Max sorted through their ornaments, deciding which ones would work best on an upside-down tree. They discovered that some ornaments, like their beloved glass icicles, looked even more magical hanging "up" from the branches.

As they worked, the house filled with the sounds of laughter and Christmas music. Even when things didn't go quite right – like when Dad accidentally tangled himself in a string of lights – they just laughed and kept going.

Finally, as the sun began to set, their masterpiece was complete. The Johnson family stood back to admire their handiwork.

There, suspended from the ceiling, was their Christmas tree. Its green branches reached down towards the floor, creating a magical canopy of pine needles and twinkling lights. Ornaments hung in unexpected places, catching the light in new and beautiful ways. And at the very bottom (which was now the top), their star shone brightly, closer to the ground than ever before.

"It's... it's beautiful," Mom breathed, her eyes shining.

Dad put his arm around her, grinning from ear to ear. "It sure is. And sturdy too! No toppling over for this tree."

Max was twirling underneath the tree, looking up in wonder. "It's like a Christmas cave!" he exclaimed.

Emma beamed with pride. Her idea had turned a potential disaster into something magical.

As they stood admiring their unique tree, there was a knock at the door. It was their neighbors, the Smiths, coming to borrow some sugar.

"Oh my goodness!" Mrs. Smith exclaimed as she caught sight of the tree. "What a wonderful idea! How creative!"

Soon, word spread through the neighborhood about the Johnsons' upside-down tree. People started dropping by just to see it, each visit filled with oohs and aahs and questions about how they did it.

The Johnsons were more than happy to explain, sharing the story of their "tree disaster" turned triumph. They served hot cocoa to their visitors and even started a new tradition of "Upside-Down Carol Singing" where everyone had to try singing carols while bending over or doing handstands. It wasn't very melodious, but it was certainly entertaining!

As Christmas approached, something wonderful happened in the neighborhood. Inspired by the Johnsons' creativity, other families started their own unique traditions.

The Garcias decorated their tree entirely with homemade ornaments. The Nguyens created a "book tree" by stacking green books in the shape of a Christmas tree. And the Clarks decided to forgo a tree altogether, instead creating a "giving tree" where they hung items to donate to those in need.

On Christmas Eve, as the Johnsons sat together under their upside-down tree, they reflected on the holiday season.

"You know, I think this has been our best Christmas yet."

Mom nodded in agreement. "It's funny how what seemed like a disaster turned into something so special."

Max looked up from where he was lying on the floor, gazing at the tree above him. "Can we do it again next year?"

Emma laughed. "Maybe! Or maybe we'll come up with a whole new idea. That's the fun part!"

As they sat there, cozy and content, they realized that Christmas wasn't about having the perfect tree or following the same traditions year after year. It was about being together, being creative, and finding joy in unexpected places.

From that year on, the Johnsons never quite knew what their Christmas tree would look like. Sometimes it was upside-down, sometimes right-side up. One year it was sideways, and another year they had a "tree" made entirely of green balloons!

But no matter what form it took, their tree was always perfect, because it was theirs, created with love, laughter, and togetherness.

So, little ones, remember the story of the upside-down Christmas tree. Sometimes, when things don't go as planned, it's an opportunity to create something even more wonderful. And the best traditions are the ones that bring you together and make you smile.

Chapter 6:
The Magical Snow Globe

In a cozy little house at the end of Evergreen Lane lived a girl named Sarah. Sarah loved everything about Christmas - the twinkling lights, the smell of gingerbread, and especially the magic that seemed to fill the air. She was always the first one up on Christmas morning, eager to see what Santa had brought.

This year, however, Sarah was feeling a little less excited than usual. Her best friend, Emma, had moved away, and Sarah was worried that Christmas wouldn't feel the same without her. She missed building snowmen and drinking hot cocoa with Emma, giggling as they tried to guess what presents they might get.

One snowy afternoon, just a week before Christmas, Sarah's grandmother came to visit. Grandma always seemed to know when Sarah needed cheering up. Her eyes twinkled with excitement as she handed Sarah a carefully wrapped package.

"This is for you, my dear," Grandma said, her voice warm and mysterious. "It's been in our family for generations, and now it's your turn to have it. I think it might be just what you need this Christmas."

Sarah carefully unwrapped the gift, her heart beating with anticipation. As the last of the paper fell away, she gasped in wonder.

In her hands was the most beautiful snowglobe she had ever seen. Inside was a miniature winter wonderland - tiny pine trees dusted with snow, a frozen lake that seemed to sparkle, and a small village with houses that looked like gingerbread cottages. There was even a minuscule clock tower in the center of the village, its hands pointing to just before midnight.

"It's beautiful, Grandma!" Sarah exclaimed, her eyes wide with delight. She gently shook the globe, watching as glittering snow swirled around the tiny world.

Grandma smiled, a knowing twinkle in her eye. "This snowglobe is very special, Sarah. They say it holds real Christmas magic. But remember, magic often works in mysterious ways. Sometimes, the things we think we've lost are just waiting to be found in unexpected places."

Sarah nodded solemnly, though she wasn't quite sure what her grandmother meant. She placed the snowglobe carefully on her bedside table, where she could see it as she fell asleep each night.

Every evening, Sarah would gently shake the snowglobe, watching in wonder as the glittering snow swirled around the tiny world inside. She imagined what it would be like to visit that magical place. Would the air smell like peppermint? Would she be able to ice skate on that perfect little frozen lake?

As she gazed into the globe, Sarah felt a little less lonely. It was as if the tiny world inside was keeping her company, reminding her of the magic of Christmas.

On Christmas Eve, as Sarah was getting ready for bed, she gave the snowglobe one last shake. But this time, something extraordinary happened.

The snowglobe began to glow with a soft, golden light. Sarah felt a strange tingling sensation in her fingers, and suddenly, she felt herself shrinking, getting smaller and smaller until...

Can you guess what happened next?

With a soft *pop*, Sarah found herself standing in the snow, surrounded by tiny pine trees. She had been magically transported inside the snowglobe!

Sarah looked around in amazement. Everything she had seen from the outside was now life-sized to her - or rather, she had shrunk to fit this miniature world. The air sparkled with falling snowflakes, and she could smell the scent of pine and cinnamon. The clock tower she had admired now loomed above her, its hands still pointing to just before midnight.

"Hello there!" a cheerful voice called out. Sarah turned to see a tiny elf, no taller than her pinky finger had been in the real world, waving at her from behind a snowbank. "You must be Sarah! We've been expecting you!"

Sarah's eyes widened in surprise. "You have? But... how?"

The elf chuckled, his laughter sounding like tinkling bells. "Why, the magic of Christmas, of course! I'm Tinsel, and we need your help. Christmas is in danger!"

Before Sarah could ask what he meant, Tinsel took her hand and led her towards the little village. As they walked, Sarah marveled at how different everything looked from this new perspective. Snowflakes that would have been tiny in her world now felt like soft, fluffy pillows gently landing on her shoulders.

They reached the village square, where a crowd of elves was gathered, all looking worried. In the center stood a very small, round man with a white beard - a miniature Santa Claus!

"Ho ho ho!" the tiny Santa said, though his usual jolly tone seemed forced. "Welcome, Sarah! We're so glad you're here."

Sarah curtsied, feeling a bit silly but not knowing what else to do. "Hello, Santa. Tinsel said Christmas is in danger. What's wrong?"

Santa sighed, his little shoulders drooping. "You see, Sarah, this snowglobe is a very important part of Christmas magic. It's connected to the real North Pole. Whatever happens here affects Christmas out in your world too. And I'm afraid we have a big problem - or should I say, a very small one."

He pointed to a nearby house, and Sarah gasped. The chimney was so narrow, it looked like a straw!

"Our chimneys have shrunk!" an elf piped up. "They're too small for Santa to go down, even at this size! If we can't fix this, Santa won't be able to deliver presents, not here and not in the big world either!"

Sarah's mind raced. This was a huge responsibility! But then she had an idea.

"What if," she said slowly, "we make the presents smaller instead of making the chimneys bigger?"

The elves looked at each other, murmuring in excitement.

"That's brilliant!" Santa exclaimed, clapping his tiny hands. "But how will we do it?"

Sarah grinned. "Leave that to me!"

And so began a night of miniature Christmas magic. Sarah taught the elves how to make tiny origami boxes for presents. They used pine needles as wrapping paper and spider silk for ribbons.

Sarah showed them how to make little toys out of acorns and twigs, creating dolls and cars so small they could fit on a fingertip. The elves were delighted, their nimble fingers perfect for this delicate work.

As they worked, Sarah learned all about life inside the snowglobe. The elves told her about their daily tasks, like painting frost on windows and teaching snowflakes how to dance. She even met the reindeer, who were no bigger than mice but could still fly with the magic of Christmas belief.

"You know," said Tinsel as they worked on a particularly tricky origami box, "we've been watching you, Sarah. We saw how sad you've been since your friend moved away."

Sarah's hands stilled. "You did?"

Tinsel nodded. "Christmas magic isn't just about presents and Santa, you know. It's about connection, about feeling close to the people we love, even when they're far away."

As if on cue, Sarah heard a familiar giggle. She turned to see a tiny version of Emma, no bigger than the elves, waving at her from across the workshop.

"Emma!" Sarah cried out in delight. "But how...?"

Emma grinned. "The same way you got here, silly! Christmas magic! I've been so worried about you, and then this snowglobe appeared in my room..."

Sarah's heart felt like it might burst with happiness. She and Emma worked side by side, catching up as they created miniature marvels. Sarah realized that even though Emma had moved away, their friendship was still as strong as ever.

As the night wore on, the pile of tiny presents grew. Sarah marveled at the intricate details they managed to create. There were miniature books with pages that really turned, tiny teddy bears with movable arms and legs, and even itty-bitty snow globes, each containing an entire winter scene no bigger than a dewdrop.

Finally, as the moon rose high in the sky (which Sarah realized was actually the curved glass top of the snowglobe), they were ready. Santa's sleigh was loaded with thousands of tiny presents, each one a miniature masterpiece.

"Thank you, Sarah," Santa said warmly. "You've saved Christmas, both here and in your world!"

Sarah beamed with pride. But as Santa prepared to take off, she felt a twinge of sadness. She didn't want to leave this magical place or say goodbye to Emma again.

As if reading her mind, Tinsel patted her hand. "Don't worry, Sarah. The magic of the snowglobe will always be with you. Whenever you look at it, remember - you're a part of this world too! And so is Emma. This globe connects you, no matter how far apart you are."

Emma nodded, giving Sarah a hug. "We can meet here anytime we want! Christmas magic, remember?"

Suddenly, Sarah felt that tingling sensation again. The world around her began to grow, or perhaps she was shrinking - it was hard to tell!

With a soft *pop*, Sarah found herself back in her bedroom, the snowglobe clutched in her hands. For a moment, she wondered if it had all been a dream.

But then she noticed something different about the snowglobe. There, in the village square, were two tiny figures that hadn't been there before - two little girls, one with Sarah's red hair and one with Emma's blonde curls, waving up at her.

Sarah smiled and waved back. She knew that whenever she looked at the snowglobe now, she'd remember her magical adventure, the Christmas she helped save, and the friend she would always be connected to, no matter the distance.

From that day on, Sarah took extra special care of the snowglobe. Every night, she'd give it a gentle shake and whisper "Merry Christmas, Emma" before going to sleep. And sometimes, if she looked very closely, she could see a tiny blonde figure waving back.

On Christmas morning, Sarah rushed downstairs to find presents under the tree, just as always. But the best gift of all was a letter from Emma, talking about a magical dream she'd had about a snowglobe and asking if Sarah had experienced anything similar.

Sarah grinned as she read the letter. She couldn't wait to write back and share their secret magical adventure.

And every Christmas Eve after that, if Sarah looked very closely at her snowglobe, she could see a tiny sleigh soaring over the miniature world, delivering joy to all - a reminder that the biggest magic often comes in the smallest packages, and that true friendship, like Christmas spirit, can span any distance.

So, little ones, the next time you see a snowglobe, look closely. You never know what kind of magic might be hiding inside. And remember, sometimes the biggest differences can be made by the smallest actions, and the strongest connections can be felt even across great distances. For in the world of Christmas magic, no one is ever truly far from those they love.

Chapter 7:
The Christmas Wish Whisper

In a small town nestled between snow-capped mountains, where icicles hung from every rooftop and the scent of pine filled the air, there lived a boy named Tommy. Tommy was different from the other children in his class. While they chattered excitedly about their Christmas wishes, filling the air with laughter and spirited debates about which toys were the best, Tommy remained silent, his words trapped behind a wall of shyness.

Tommy's parents, Mr. and Mrs. Anderson, worried about their son. They'd tried everything to help him overcome his shyness - encouraging him to join clubs, arranging playdates, even considering speech therapy. But nothing seemed to work. Tommy would just curl up with a book or lose himself in drawing, his voice rarely rising above a whisper.

As Christmas approached, the town buzzed with excitement. Colorful lights adorned every house, and a giant Christmas tree stood proudly in the town square. In Tommy's classroom, the excitement was palpable. Miss Maple, Tommy's kind-hearted teacher, announced a special project with a warm smile that crinkled the corners of her eyes.

"Children," she said, her voice filled with enthusiasm, "tomorrow, we'll be writing letters to Santa about our Christmas wishes!"

The classroom erupted in excited chatter. "I'm asking for a new bike!" shouted Jimmy from the back. "I want a dollhouse!" exclaimed Sarah, bouncing in her seat.

But Tommy's heart sank, a heavy feeling settling in his stomach. How could he write about his wishes when he could barely speak them aloud? The thought of having to share his letter with the class made his palms sweat and his throat tighten.

That night, as snowflakes danced outside his window like tiny ballerinas in a winter ballet, Tommy lay in bed, worry creasing his young brow. He could hear his parents talking in low voices downstairs, probably discussing their quiet son yet again.

"I wish I could tell someone what I want for Christmas," he whispered so softly that even he could barely hear it. "I wish I wasn't so afraid to speak up."

Suddenly, a cool breeze swept through the room, despite the closed window. It swirled around Tommy, carrying the scent of peppermint and pine, with just a hint of cinnamon. The curtains rustled gently, and the pages of Tommy's storybook fluttered. And then, to Tommy's amazement, the breeze began to speak!

"Hello, Tommy," it whispered, its voice like the rustle of wrapping paper. "I'm the Wish Whisper, and I've come to help you."

Tommy sat up in bed, his eyes wide with wonder and a touch of fear. "Are... are you magic?" he managed to stammer, his voice barely audible.

The Wish Whisper chuckled, a sound like tinkling icicles. "I'm Christmas magic, Tommy. I heard your wish, and I'm here to help you share it. Every year, I seek out children who need a little extra help finding their voice."

Tommy hugged his knees to his chest, both excited and nervous. "But how can you help me? I've always been shy. I don't know how to speak up."

"With practice," the Wish Whisper replied gently. "Let's start small. Whisper your wish to me, Tommy. Don't worry, no one else will hear."

Hesitantly, Tommy leaned forward and whispered his Christmas wish, so quietly that it was almost inaudible. But the Wish Whisper heard.

"That's a wonderful wish, Tommy!" it exclaimed. "Now, let's work on making your whisper a little stronger. Remember, your voice is like a muscle. The more you use it, the stronger it gets."

All night, the Wish Whisper stayed with Tommy, encouraging him to speak his wish a little louder each time. They practiced different ways of saying it - as a question, as an exclamation, even singing it softly. By morning, Tommy could say his wish in a soft but clear voice.

At school, Tommy clutched his pencil, staring at the blank paper before him. The classroom buzzed with activity as his classmates scribbled their letters furiously, their excitement almost tangible. Tommy felt a knot of anxiety in his stomach, but then he remembered the Wish Whisper's encouragement. Taking a deep breath, he began to write.

Miss Maple noticed Tommy working diligently and smiled to herself. She had always had a soft spot for the quiet boy, recognizing the bright mind behind his shy exterior. When it was time to share, she gently asked, "Tommy, would you like to read your letter?"

Tommy hesitated, his heart pounding so loudly he was sure everyone could hear it. But then he felt a familiar cool breeze ruffle his hair. Taking another deep breath, he stood up and, in a voice that started as a whisper but grew stronger with each word, read his letter.

"Dear Santa," he read, his voice trembling slightly at first, "for Christmas, I wish for the courage to speak up and make new friends. I have a lot of thoughts and ideas, but I'm often too scared to share them. I want to be brave enough to raise my hand in class, to tell jokes at lunch, and to ask others to play with me at recess. I think if I could do that, it would be the best gift ever."

The classroom was silent for a moment, then erupted in applause. Tommy's classmates, who had never heard him speak so much before, were amazed and touched by his honest wish. Miss Maple had tears in her eyes, proud of the enormous step Tommy had taken.

"That's a beautiful wish, Tommy," she said warmly. "Thank you for sharing it with us."

As Tommy sat down, he felt a warmth spreading through him. For the first time, he felt truly heard.

Encouraged by this success, the Wish Whisper had an idea. That night, as Tommy lay in bed still glowing from his accomplishment, the magical breeze returned.

"Tommy," it whispered, "there are other children who find it hard to share their wishes. Would you like to help them?"

Tommy nodded eagerly, excited by the idea of helping others like himself.

And so began a magical adventure. Each night, the Wish Whisper would take Tommy (in his dreams, of course) to visit other shy children. Together, they would encourage these children to voice their wishes.

There was Sarah, a girl in the next town over, who whispered her wish for a puppy so quietly that her parents had never heard. With Tommy and the Wish Whisper's encouragement, she found the courage to tell her family, leading to a joyful Christmas morning surprise.

Then there was Miguel, a boy in Tommy's school who wanted to join the choir but was too afraid to audition. Tommy shared his own story, inspiring Miguel to sign up. When Miguel's clear, beautiful voice rang out in the Christmas concert, Tommy felt a surge of pride.

As Christmas drew nearer, Tommy's confidence grew. He started talking more in class, even raising his hand to answer questions. His classmates, charmed by his gentle nature and insightful comments, eagerly included him in their games and conversations.

But Tommy's greatest challenge was yet to come. The school's Christmas pageant was approaching, and Miss Maple was looking for someone to play the role of the Christmas Star – a role that required delivering a short speech in front of the entire school and their families.

"Would you like to try, Tommy?" Miss Maple asked kindly after class one day. "I think you'd be perfect for the role."

Tommy felt a flutter of panic, his old shyness threatening to overwhelm him. But then he heard the Wish Whisper's encouraging rustle. Slowly, he nodded. "I'll try," he said, his voice small but determined.

For the next week, Tommy practiced his lines tirelessly. He recited them in front of his mirror, to his parents, even to his dog, Max. The Wish Whisper was always there, cheering him on, reminding him of how far he'd come.

On the night of the pageant, the school auditorium was packed. Parents, grandparents, and siblings filled every seat, their excitement palpable. Backstage, Tommy peeked out from behind the curtain, his heart racing. What if he forgot his lines? What if his voice failed him?

Just then, he felt the familiar cool breeze of the Wish Whisper. "Remember, Tommy," it whispered, "your voice is a gift. Share it with the world. And remember all the other children you've helped. They're out there, and they believe in you."

As Tommy stepped onto the stage, dressed in a glittering star costume, he saw his parents in the audience, their faces shining with pride. He took a deep breath and began to speak.

"I am the Christmas Star," he said, his voice clear and strong, ringing out across the hushed auditorium. "I shine for all to see, a beacon of hope and joy. I remind us that even in the darkest night, there is light. And in the quietest heart, there is a voice waiting to be heard."

As Tommy continued his speech, he felt as if he was wrapped in the Wish Whisper's gentle breeze, giving him strength and courage. He spoke of the magic of Christmas, of the power of wishes, and of the importance of every voice, no matter how small.

When he finished, there was a moment of awed silence. Then the audience burst into applause. Tommy's parents had tears in their eyes, and his classmates cheered loudly. Miss Maple was beaming with pride. Tommy felt a warmth spread through him – the warmth of accomplishment, of being truly heard.

As Christmas Eve arrived, Tommy sat by his window, watching the stars twinkle. The past few weeks had changed him in ways he never thought possible. He had found his voice, made new friends, and even helped other children overcome their own shyness.

"Thank you, Wish Whisper," he said, his voice confident and clear. "You've given me the best Christmas gift ever."

The Wish Whisper swirled around him one last time. "No, Tommy," it replied. "You've given yourself this gift. Your voice was always there – you just needed to believe in it. And now, you've helped others find their voices too. That's the true magic of Christmas."

Tommy smiled, feeling a sense of peace and joy he'd never experienced before. He knew that even though the Wish Whisper might not always be with him, the courage and confidence he'd gained would stay with him always.

From that Christmas on, Tommy became known as someone who could always lend an ear – and a voice – to those who struggled to express themselves. He started a club at school for shy children, creating a safe space for them to practice speaking up. And on quiet winter nights, if you listen very carefully, you might just hear the Wish Whisper, encouraging those who need a little help to share their dreams.

So, little ones, remember Tommy's story. Your voice, no matter how small, has the power to make a big difference. And sometimes, the quietest whisper can lead to the loudest cheer. All you need is a little courage, a little magic, and the belief that your words matter. For in every heart, there's a wish waiting to be whispered, and in every whisper, there's the potential to change the world.

Chapter 8:
Santa's High-Tech Mishap

Up at the North Pole, where the northern lights dance across the sky and the snow sparkles like diamond dust, Santa's workshop buzzed with activity. Santa had decided it was time for an upgrade. "Ho ho ho!" he announced to his elves one chilly morning. "We're going to modernize the workshop! Bring Christmas into the 21st century!"

The elves exchanged worried glances. They loved their traditional ways of making toys and organizing gifts. But Santa was the boss, and his eyes were twinkling with excitement.

"Just think," Santa continued, his cheeks rosy with enthusiasm, "we'll have robots to help wrap presents, computers to sort the naughty and nice lists, and even a GPS system for the sleigh!"

And so, over the next few months, Santa's workshop transformed. Shiny machines appeared alongside workbenches. Computers hummed in corners where elves used to sit and paint toy soldiers. Even Santa's big book of children's names was replaced by a sleek tablet.

At first, things seemed to be going well. The robot gift-wrappers could wrap presents at lightning speed. The computer system organized the naughty and nice lists in seconds. Santa was delighted.

"You see?" he said to Mrs. Claus, who was eyeing the changes with suspicion. "This is the future of Christmas!"

But as Christmas Eve drew near, strange things started to happen.

It began with the present-wrapping robots. Instead of festive paper and ribbons, they started using old newspaper and packing tape.

"Oh dear," said Jingle, the head elf of the wrapping department. "I think there's a glitch in their programming!"

Next, the computer system for sorting gifts went haywire. Instead of matching presents to children's wishes, it started categorizing them by color and shape.

"Santa!" called Twinkle, the elf in charge of gift assignments. "The computer thinks all the red gifts should go to children whose names start with 'R'!"

But the real trouble came on Christmas Eve itself. As Santa prepared for his big night, he decided to test the new GPS system in his sleigh.

"No more getting lost in fog!" he chuckled, inputting his route into the sleek device.

The reindeer, who prided themselves on their excellent sense of direction, snorted in disapproval.

As Santa took off into the night sky, things seemed fine at first. But soon, the GPS started to act strangely.

"Turn left at the next cloud," it instructed in a robotic voice.

"Left?" Santa frowned. "But the first stop is to the right!"

Confused, Santa followed the GPS's directions. But instead of arriving at little Timmy's house in New York, he found himself hovering over a penguin colony in Antarctica.

"Oh, Christmas cookies!" Santa exclaimed. "This won't do at all!"

He tried to override the system, but it was no use. The GPS had taken control of the sleigh's navigation.

For the next hour, Santa was led on a wild goose chase around the globe. He found himself at the top of Mount Everest, in the middle of the Sahara Desert, and even circling the Eiffel Tower.

Meanwhile, back at the North Pole, the elves were in a panic. The present-wrapping robots had run amok, turning the workshop into a sea of mismatched paper and tangled ribbons. The gift-sorting computer had crashed, spewing out garbled lists of names and presents.

Mrs. Claus, seeing the chaos, decided to take charge. "Alright, everyone," she called out, her voice calm but firm. "It's time to do things the old-fashioned way!"

With a flick of a switch, she shut down all the high-tech gadgets. The elves cheered and quickly got to work, their nimble hands wrapping presents and sorting gifts with practiced ease.

But what about Santa? He was still zooming around the world, following the haywire GPS.

"Dasher, Dancer, Prancer, Vixen!" Santa called out to his reindeer. "We need to find our way home!"

The reindeer, glad to finally be useful, took control. With their innate sense of direction, they steered the sleigh back towards the North Pole.

As they approached the workshop, Santa's heart sank. It was nearly midnight, and not a single present had been delivered. Christmas was ruined!

But as they landed, Santa was met with an amazing sight. The elves had worked faster than ever before, wrapping and sorting all the presents by hand. Mrs. Claus stood at the head of an organized line of elves, each holding a bag of gifts.

"We're ready, Santa!" she called out. "And we've got a plan!"

Quickly, Mrs. Claus explained how they had divided the world into sections, with teams of elves ready to accompany Santa on multiple trips. It would be a long night, but they could still deliver all the presents before sunrise.

Santa's eyes filled with tears of gratitude. "Oh, what would I do without you all?" he said, giving Mrs. Claus a big hug.

And so, they set off. Santa and his team of elves made trip after trip, delivering presents around the world. Without the high-tech gadgets slowing them down, they worked faster and more efficiently than ever before.

As the first light of dawn began to color the sky, Santa and his helpers returned to the North Pole, tired but triumphant. Every last present had been delivered, every stocking had been filled.

"I've learned an important lesson," Santa said to all gathered in the workshop. "Sometimes, the old ways are the best ways. It's not the gadgets that make Christmas magical – it's all of you, with your hard work, quick thinking, and Christmas spirit."

The elves cheered, and even the reindeer let out happy snorts.

From that day on, Santa's workshop returned to its traditional ways. The robots were reprogrammed to help with heavy lifting, the computers were used for sending cheerful emails to children, and the GPS... well, it made a very nice paperweight on Santa's desk.

But Santa didn't abandon technology completely. He knew that the modern world was always changing, and Christmas had to keep up in some ways. So he found a balance, blending a bit of new with the tried-and-true old.

The next year, as Santa prepared for his Christmas Eve journey, he smiled at his workshop. Elves cheerfully wrapped presents by hand, checked the lists in big books, and loaded the sleigh using good old-fashioned teamwork. But there was also a fancy new hot chocolate machine keeping everyone warm, and a magical device that let the elves video chat with children around the world.

As he took off into the night sky, guided by Rudolph's shining nose, Santa chuckled to himself. "Merry Christmas to all," he called out, his voice carrying on the winter wind. "And to all a good night – no batteries required!"

Chapter 9:
The Grumpy Gingerbread Man

In a cozy kitchen, where the air was always filled with the scent of cinnamon and sugar, there lived a gingerbread man named Snap. But Snap wasn't like other gingerbread men. Oh no, Snap was grumpy.

You see, Snap had a problem. Every time someone saw him, they wanted to eat him!

"It's not fair," Snap would grumble as he dodged grabbing hands. "I have feelings too, you know!"

Mrs. Bakewell, the kindly old lady who had baked Snap, didn't understand why he was always so cross. She had given him a cheerful smile made of icing and bright gumdrop buttons. But no matter how she decorated him, Snap's frosting eyebrows were always furrowed in a frown.

One day, as Christmas approached, Mrs. Bakewell decided to bake a whole batch of gingerbread friends for Snap. "Maybe some company will cheer him up," she thought.

But when the new gingerbread people came out of the oven, Snap just huffed. "Great, more people to try and eat me," he muttered.

The other gingerbread folk were confused by Snap's attitude. They tried to include him in their games, sliding down the kitchen counter and playing hide-and-seek in the cookie jar. But Snap always refused.

"Don't you know we're all going to be eaten eventually?" he'd say. "What's the point of having fun?"

As Christmas Eve drew near, Mrs. Bakewell began preparing for the annual town Christmas fair. She carefully placed all the gingerbread people in a beautiful display box, ready to be sold at her booth.

Snap was horrified. "Sold? You mean... eaten?" he gasped.

Mrs. Bakewell patted his head gently. "Now, now, Snap. Bringing joy to others is what Christmas is all about. You'll see."

But Snap didn't want to see. That night, when everyone was asleep, he made a decision. He was going to run away!

Carefully, he pushed open the box lid and climbed out. He tiptoed past the sleeping cat and slipped under the front door, out into the snowy night.

The world outside was cold and dark, nothing like the warm, sweet-smelling kitchen. Snap shivered, his gingerbread legs trembling in the frosty air. But he was determined. "At least out here, nobody will try to eat me," he thought.

Snap wandered through the quiet town, marveling at the twinkling Christmas lights and the colorful decorations. Despite his grumpiness, he couldn't help but feel a tiny spark of wonder.

As he turned a corner, he heard a small, sad sound. There, huddled in a doorway, was a tiny mouse, shivering in the cold.

"Are you okay?" Snap asked, surprising himself with his concern.

The mouse looked up, its eyes wide. "I'm so cold and hungry," it squeaked. "I can't find any food in this weather."

Snap felt a strange feeling in his gingerbread heart. Before he knew what he was doing, he broke off one of his gumdrop buttons and offered it to the mouse.

"Here," he said gruffly. "It's not much, but it's something."

The mouse's eyes lit up with joy. "Oh, thank you!" it cried, nibbling on the gumdrop. "You've saved my life!"

As Snap watched the mouse enjoy the tiny treat, he felt something he'd never experienced before - the warmth of giving.

Encouraged by this new feeling, Snap continued his journey. He came across a family of snowbirds, their feathers ruffled by the cold wind. Without hesitation, he broke off a piece of his arm and crumbled it for them to eat.

"Merry Christmas," he said, a small smile tugging at his icing mouth.

The birds chirped happily, pecking at the sweet crumbs. "Thank you, kind gingerbread man!" they sang.

As the night went on, Snap encountered more and more creatures in need. A squirrel with empty food stores for the winter. A stray kitten, lost and hungry. Each time, Snap shared a piece of himself, and each time, his heart grew a little warmer.

By the time dawn broke on Christmas morning, Snap had given away most of himself. He was missing an arm, a leg, and all his buttons. But strangely, he didn't feel grumpy anymore. In fact, he felt happier than he ever had before.

As the sun rose, Snap found himself back at Mrs. Bakewell's house. He was tired and broken, but his icing smile was wide and genuine.

Mrs. Bakewell opened the door, her eyes widening in surprise when she saw him. "Snap! Where have you been? We've been so worried!"

Snap looked up at her, his gingerbread face beaming. "I'm sorry I ran away," he said. "But I learned something important. Giving a part of yourself to others... that's what makes life sweet."

Mrs. Bakewell's eyes filled with tears of joy. She gently picked Snap up and brought him inside, where the other gingerbread folk welcomed him with cheers and hugs.

From that day on, Snap was a changed gingerbread man. He no longer feared being eaten, because he had discovered the joy of giving. At the

Christmas fair, he asked to be broken into tiny pieces, so that as many people as possible could enjoy him.

And as each person tasted a bit of Snap, they felt a warmth in their heart - the warmth of his kindness and generosity.

The tale of the grumpy gingerbread man who learned to love giving became a beloved Christmas story in the town. Every year, Mrs. Bakewell would bake a special gingerbread man named Snap, and children would line up to receive a small piece, reminding them of the sweetness of sharing.

So, little ones, remember Snap's story. Sometimes, the thing we fear the most can lead us to our greatest joy. And in giving, we often receive the most precious gift of all - the warmth of kindness in our hearts.

Chapter 10:
The Lost Christmas Carol

In the quaint town of Harmony Grove, where cobblestone streets wound between gingerbread-trimmed houses, there was a peculiar problem. As December arrived and the townsfolk began their Christmas preparations, they realized something was missing. The usual joy that filled the air seemed muted, as if a vital ingredient had been left out of their holiday recipe.

It was young Emily Watson, a bright-eyed girl with a passion for music, who first put her finger on the problem. "Mom," she said one evening as they hung stockings by the fireplace, "why aren't we singing the Harmony Grove Christmas carol this year?"

Her mother, Sarah, paused, a puzzled look crossing her face. "You know, I'm not sure. Come to think of it, I can't quite remember how it goes."

This conversation sparked a town-wide realization. Harmony Grove had always had its own special Christmas carol, a song that had been passed down through generations. But somehow, someway, the town had forgotten it.

Mayor Appleby called an emergency town meeting. The community gathered in the old town hall, their voices a mix of concern and confusion.

"Friends," the mayor announced, his bushy eyebrows furrowed with worry, "it seems our beloved town carol has been lost. Does anyone remember how it goes?"

The room filled with murmurs. Old Mrs. Finch hummed a few notes, but then shook her head. "No, that's 'Jingle Bells,'" she sighed.

Mr. Jones, the music teacher, tried to recall the lyrics, but could only remember something about snowflakes and candlelight.

As the meeting ended without a solution, Emily had an idea. "What if," she suggested to her parents, "we try to piece the carol back together? Like a musical puzzle!"

Emily's enthusiasm was contagious. Soon, a plan was formed. The children of Harmony Grove would interview the town's elderly residents, collecting fragments of memories about the lost carol. Then, they'd work with Mr. Jones to reconstruct the song.

The next day, Emily and her friends set out on their mission. They visited the Sunshine Retirement Home, armed with notepads and unbridled curiosity.

Their first interview was with Old Tom, a former postman known for his sharp memory. "The carol," he mused, stroking his white beard, "I remember it had something about bells in it. Silver bells, ringing clear on Christmas Eve."

Emily scribbled furiously in her notepad, her eyes shining with excitement.

Next, they spoke to Granny Rose, who used to run the town bakery. "Oh, the carol!" she exclaimed, her wrinkled face lighting up. "It mentioned the scent of pine and cinnamon in the air. And something about starlight reflecting off the snow."

With each interview, more pieces of the puzzle emerged. Miss Lily, a retired schoolteacher, recalled a line about children's laughter echoing through the town. Mr. Carpenter, who had once been the town's clockmaker, remembered a verse about time standing still on Christmas night.

As the children gathered their notes, a picture began to form. The lost carol wasn't just a song – it was a story of Harmony Grove itself, capturing the essence of their Christmas traditions and the spirit of their community.

Back at school, Mr. Jones pored over the children's findings. "This is remarkable," he said, his eyes twinkling behind his spectacles. "With this, I think we can reconstruct the melody and lyrics!"

For the next week, the school was abuzz with activity. Children hummed potential tunes in the hallways, and impromptu lyric-writing sessions broke out during lunch breaks. Mr. Jones worked tirelessly, piecing together the musical fragments like a conductor assembling an orchestra.

Finally, on a snowy evening a week before Christmas, the town gathered once again in the hall. The air was thick with anticipation as Mr. Jones stepped onto the stage, followed by Emily and the school choir.

"Ladies and gentlemen," Mr. Jones announced, "thanks to the hard work of our young detectives and the cherished memories of our eldest residents, I believe we have reconstructed the Harmony Grove Christmas Carol. Emily will lead us in singing it."

A hush fell over the crowd as Emily stepped forward. Her clear voice rang out, singing of silver bells and starlit snow, of the scent of pine and cinnamon, and of the timeless magic of Christmas in their beloved town.

As the familiar words and melody filled the air, something magical happened. One by one, the townspeople began to join in. It was as if the song had awakened a sleeping memory in their hearts. Voices young and old blended together, growing stronger with each verse.

By the final chorus, the entire town was singing, their voices rising in perfect harmony. Tears glistened in many eyes, and smiles adorned every face. The lost carol had been found, and with it, the true spirit of Christmas in Harmony Grove had been rediscovered.

As the last notes faded away, the town hall erupted in cheers and applause. Mayor Appleby, wiping a tear from his eye, stepped onto the stage.

"My dear friends," he said, his voice thick with emotion, "tonight, we have reclaimed more than just a song. We have rediscovered the heart of our community. This carol is a reminder of who we are and what makes our town special."

From that night on, the Harmony Grove Christmas Carol became more precious than ever. The town vowed to sing it every day during the holiday season, ensuring it would never be forgotten again.

Emily's idea had not only saved the carol but had brought the community closer together. The interviews with the elderly residents had sparked new friendships between the youngest and oldest members of the town. Stories and traditions that had almost been lost were now being shared and celebrated.

As Christmas Eve arrived, the town gathered in the square for their annual tree lighting ceremony. But this year, something was different. Before the lights were switched on, Emily stepped forward, holding a small, leather-bound book.

"This book," she announced, her voice carrying clearly through the crisp winter air, "contains our carol, along with all the stories and memories we collected. It's our town's Christmas legacy, and every year, we'll add new verses and new memories to it."

The crowd murmured in approval as Emily handed the book to Mayor Appleby for safekeeping. Then, as the magnificent tree lit up, bathing the square in a warm glow, the townspeople joined hands and began to sing their beloved carol once more.

The sound of their voices, rising in perfect harmony, seemed to make the very stars twinkle brighter. At that moment, everyone in Harmony Grove felt the true magic of Christmas – the power of tradition, the strength of community, and the joy of raising their voices together in song.

So, little ones, remember the story of the lost Christmas carol. It teaches us that the most precious melodies are the ones that live in our hearts, connecting us to our past and to each other. And sometimes, it takes the curiosity of the young and the wisdom of the old to rediscover the music that makes our spirits soar.

Chapter 11:
Mittens for Everyone

❧

In the small town of Frostville, where icicles hung from every rooftop and the snow piled high on every doorstep, lived a little girl named Lily. Lily was known throughout her school for two things: her bright red hair that looked like a cheerful flame in the winter landscape, and her enormous heart that seemed too big for her small body.

Lily's most prized possession was a pair of mittens her grandmother had knitted for her before she passed away last winter. They were soft as clouds and warm as a hug, decorated with tiny snowflakes in sparkling silver thread. Lily loved these mittens more than anything in the world, not just for their warmth, but for the love they represented.

One particularly cold December day, as Lily was getting ready for recess, she noticed her classmate, Tommy, looking sadly at his bare hands. Tommy was new to the school, having just moved to Frostville, and Lily remembered overhearing that his family was going through some tough times.

Without hesitation, Lily approached Tommy. "Hi Tommy," she said softly. "Are your hands cold?"

Tommy nodded, his eyes downcast. "I forgot my mittens today," he mumbled, though Lily suspected there was more to the story.

Lily looked down at her beloved mittens, then back at Tommy's red, chapped hands. In that moment, she made a decision that would change Frostville Elementary School forever.

"Here," she said, pulling off her mittens and holding them out to Tommy. "Please take these. Your hands need them more than mine do today."

Tommy's eyes widened in surprise. "Oh, no, Lily, I couldn't—"

But Lily insisted, gently placing the mittens in his hands. "Please," she said. "It would make me happy to know your hands are warm. My grandma always said that warm hands make a warm heart, and everyone deserves a warm heart at Christmas."

Reluctantly, Tommy slipped on the mittens. His face immediately relaxed as warmth spread through his fingers. "Thank you," he whispered, his eyes bright with gratitude. "That's really kind of you, Lily."

As they headed out to the snowy playground, Lily's hands were cold, but her heart was warm. Watching Tommy laughing and playing, able to enjoy the snow like the other kids, Lily had an idea. If one pair of mittens could bring so much joy, what if every kid who needed them had a pair?

That afternoon, as she walked home from school with her best friend Emma, Lily shared her idea. "What if," she said excitedly, "we could make mittens for all the kids who need them? Not just at our school, but maybe even other schools too!"

Emma's eyes lit up. "That's a great idea, Lily! But how would we do it?"

Lily's mind was already racing with possibilities. "We could learn to knit, like my grandma taught me. And maybe we could ask for help – from our families, our teachers, maybe even other students!"

By the time they reached Lily's house, the girls had the beginnings of a plan. Lily couldn't wait to tell her parents about her idea to warm hands and hearts all over Frostville.

Certainly! I'll continue with the rest of the revised "Mittens for Everyone" story:

That evening, Lily excitedly shared her idea with her parents. "Mom, Dad, I want to make mittens for kids who need them!" she exclaimed, her eyes shining with enthusiasm.

Her parents exchanged proud glances. "That's a wonderful idea, sweetie," her mother said. "How can we help?"

With her parents' support, Lily's project quickly took shape. Her mother taught her and Emma how to knit, just as Lily's grandmother had done. Her father helped them create posters to put up around the school, announcing their "Mittens for All" project.

The next day, Lily and Emma presented their idea to their teacher, Ms. Thompson. "What a lovely thought," Ms. Thompson said, beaming. "Why don't you tell the whole class about it?"

Standing in front of her classmates, Lily felt a flutter of nerves. But when she saw Tommy smiling encouragingly, still wearing her grandmother's mittens, she found her courage.

"We want to make sure every kid has warm mittens this winter," Lily explained. "We're going to knit them ourselves, and we'd love your help!"

To Lily's delight, her classmates were excited about the idea. Some, like Lily, wanted to learn to knit. Others offered to bring in yarn or old mittens that could be unraveled and re-knitted. Even the boys, who initially thought knitting was "just for girls," got involved when Ms. Thompson showed them how to use looms to make simple mittens.

The project quickly spread beyond their classroom. Other teachers heard about it and wanted their classes to participate too. The art teacher offered to help students design colorful patterns. The math teacher turned it into a lesson, helping students calculate how much yarn they'd need and how many mittens they could make.

As word spread, the whole community began to get involved. The local craft store donated baskets of colorful yarn. Parents and grandparents volunteered to teach knitting classes after school. Even the town's knitting club got involved, their experienced hands working quickly to add to the growing pile of mittens.

Lily was amazed at how her small idea had grown. Every day after school, she and Emma would meet with other students to knit and chat. Lily loved seeing her classmates work together, helping each other learn and laughing over dropped stitches.

As Christmas approached, the mittens began to pile up. There were mittens of every color and size, some perfectly knitted, others a bit lumpy but made with love. Lily's heart swelled with pride every time she looked at them.

Finally, the day came to distribute the mittens. Lily and her friends carefully wrapped each pair, attaching a small note that read, "Warm hands, warm heart. Happy Holidays from your friends at Frostville Elementary."

With the help of their teachers and parents, they delivered mittens to every child in their school who needed them. But they didn't stop there. They had made so many mittens that they were able to donate pairs to other schools in the district and even to the local children's shelter.

On the last day of school before Christmas break, Lily saw Tommy on the playground. He was wearing a new pair of mittens – ones he had made himself in their after-school knitting group.

"Lily!" he called out, waving. "Look what I made! And guess what? I'm going to teach my little sister how to make mittens too!"

Lily grinned, her heart full of joy. Her simple act of kindness had grown into something amazing, warming not just hands, but hearts throughout Frostville.

That night, as Lily hung her own mittens by the fireplace, she thought about all the children who would be warm this winter because of their project. She realized that the best gift she had received this Christmas wasn't something she could unwrap – it was the joy of giving and the warmth of community.

As she drifted off to sleep, Lily smiled, already dreaming of next year's "Mittens for All" project. Maybe they could make scarves too!

So, little ones, remember Lily's story. It shows us that even the smallest act of kindness can grow into something wonderful. And sometimes, the best gift we can give is the warmth of our own hearts, shared with others. For in the end, it's not the mittens that keep us warmest, but the love and kindness we share with one another.

Chapter 12:
The Star on Top

In the cozy attic of the Johnson family home, where dust motes danced in beams of winter sunlight, a group of Christmas ornaments waited eagerly for their yearly moment of glory. It was December 1st, and soon they would be brought down to decorate the family's Christmas tree.

Among the ornaments was a dazzling array of characters: there was Glitter, a shimmering glass ball who loved to catch the light; Chip, an old-fashioned wooden soldier with a slightly chipped hat; Ribbon, a cheerful red bow who prided herself on her perfect loops; and Jingle, a merry little bell with the sweetest ring.

But the most treasured ornament of all was Stella, a beautiful golden star. For as long as anyone could remember, Stella had always had the honor of sitting atop the Christmas tree, crowning it with her radiant glow.

As the sound of footsteps on the attic stairs grew louder, the ornaments quivered with excitement.

"This is it, everyone!" Glitter exclaimed, her surface shimmering. "Our time to shine!"

The attic door creaked open, and Mr. Johnson appeared, followed by his children, Emma and Max.

"Alright, kids," Mr. Johnson said, reaching for the first box of decorations. "Let's get these downstairs and start decorating!"

As the Johnsons carried the boxes down, the ornaments chattered excitedly among themselves.

"Oh, I do hope I get placed near the lights this year," Glitter said. "They make me sparkle so beautifully!"

"I just want to be hung securely," Chip said with a chuckle. "These old joints aren't what they used to be!"

But as they were carried down to the living room, something unprecedented happened. Mr. Johnson stumbled slightly, and Stella tumbled out of her protective wrapping, landing with a soft thud on the carpet.

"Oh no!" Emma cried, quickly picking up the star. "Dad, look! Stella's point is bent!"

Mr. Johnson examined the star closely. "You're right, sweetie. I'm not sure we can fix this in time for decorating. We might need to get a new topper this year."

A collective gasp went through the box of ornaments. No Stella on top? It was unthinkable!

As the Johnsons began to decorate the tree, the ornaments found themselves in an unfamiliar situation. For the first time in memory, the position of tree topper was up for grabs.

"Well," said Glitter, puffing up importantly, "I suppose I could take on the role of tree topper. My sparkle would look magnificent from up there!"

"Now hold on," Chip interjected. "I may be old, but I'm sturdy. The top of the tree needs someone dependable."

"Oh, please," Ribbon scoffed. "Clearly, a bow is the perfect topper. I'm festive and lightweight!"

"What about me?" Jingle chimed in. "I could ring out the Christmas cheer from the very top!"

And so began the great tree topper debate. Each ornament was convinced they were the best choice, and soon their friendly discussion turned into a heated argument.

"You're too heavy, Chip! You'll make the tree tip over!"

"Well, you're too light, Ribbon! A strong breeze would knock you right off!"

"At least I don't blind everyone who looks at me, Glitter!"

"Hey, watch who you're calling blinding, you loud little bell!"

The bickering continued as the Johnsons decorated the lower branches of the tree. Ornaments were hung with care, tinsel was draped gracefully, and lights twinkled merrily. But still, the top of the tree remained bare, and the argument raged on.

It was Stella, lying forgotten on a side table, who finally spoke up. "Friends, friends!" she called out, her voice soft but firm. "Listen to yourselves! This isn't what Christmas is about!"

The ornaments fell silent, looking sheepishly at Stella.

"But Stella," Glitter said, "we were just trying to help. The tree needs a topper!"

Stella smiled gently. "The tree doesn't need a topper to be beautiful. Look at yourselves - each of you brings something special to the tree. Glitter, your sparkle adds magic to every branch. Chip, your steadfast presence reminds us of cherished traditions. Ribbon, your festive spirit brightens the whole room. And Jingle, your sweet sound fills the air with joy."

The ornaments looked at each other, beginning to see the truth in Stella's words.

"We're all important," Stella continued. "It's not about being on top. It's about coming together to create something beautiful. That's the real magic of Christmas."

As Stella's words sank in, a remarkable thing began to happen. The ornaments started to glow with a warm, golden light - the same light that had always shone from Stella. It was as if her Christmas spirit had spread to each of them.

Just then, Emma noticed the glowing tree. "Dad, look!" she gasped. "It's so beautiful!"

The Johnsons gathered around the tree, marveling at the warm glow emanating from every ornament.

"It's magical," Mrs. Johnson whispered. "I've never seen anything like it!"

Max, the youngest, pointed to the top of the tree. "But what about the star?" he asked.

Mr. Johnson looked thoughtful for a moment, then smiled. "You know what? I think this year, our tree doesn't need a topper. It's perfect just the way it is."

The family stood back, admiring their unique and beautifully glowing tree. And up in the branches, the ornaments shared knowing smiles, their argument long forgotten in the warm glow of togetherness.

From that year on, the Johnsons' Christmas tree became famous in the neighborhood. People would come from all around to see the tree that glowed from within, topped not by a single star, but crowned by the collective spirit of all the ornaments.

And Stella? Well, she was given a place of honor on the mantelpiece, where she could watch over her friends and remind everyone of the true meaning of Christmas - that it's not about being on top, but about lifting each other up and shining together.

As for the ornaments, they never argued about their positions again. Instead, they looked forward to working together each year to create the most magical tree possible. They had learned that when everyone contributes their own special light, the result is far more beautiful than any single star could ever be.

So, little ones, remember the story of Stella and her friends. It teaches us that true beauty comes not from outshining others, but from shining together. In life, as on the Christmas tree, it's not about being on top - it's about bringing out the best in one another and creating something wonderful together.

Chapter 13:
The Last-Minute Christmas Tree

It was Christmas Eve in the little town of Pine Valley, and the Bennett family was in a panic. They had been so busy with work, school, and holiday preparations that they had forgotten the most important decoration of all – the Christmas tree!

"How could we forget the tree?" Mrs. Bennett exclaimed, wringing her hands as she looked at the bare corner of their living room.

Mr. Bennett scratched his head, looking out the window at the swirling snow. "The tree lot in town will be closed by now," he said with a sigh.

Twelve-year-old Emma and her little brother Jack exchanged worried glances. Christmas without a tree? It was unthinkable!

"Maybe we could make one?" Jack suggested, his eyes lighting up with the kind of creative energy only a seven-year-old could muster on Christmas Eve.

Emma was about to dismiss the idea when she paused. "You know, Jack might be onto something. We can't get a real tree, but maybe we can create something special of our own."

Their parents looked skeptical but hopeful. "What did you have in mind, sweetie?" Mrs. Bennett asked.

Emma's mind was already racing. "We'll need everyone's help, and we'll have to use whatever we can find around the house. But I think we can do it!"

And so, on a snowy Christmas Eve, the Bennett family embarked on a mission to create a last-minute Christmas tree that would save their holiday...

The Bennetts sprang into action, determined to create a Christmas tree before midnight. Emma took charge, her mind buzzing with ideas.

"Mom, do we have any green fabric?" she asked.

Mrs. Bennett nodded, "I think there's some in my sewing box. What are you thinking?"

"We're going to make a tree-shaped tapestry," Emma explained. "Dad, can you help us move the bookshelf to the corner?"

Mr. Bennett and Jack carefully shifted the tall bookshelf to the perfect spot. Meanwhile, Emma and her mother spread out the green fabric on the living room floor.

"Now," Emma said, "let's cut it into a big triangle shape."

As they worked, Jack's eyes lit up. "I know! We can use my building blocks to make the trunk!"

"That's brilliant, Jack!" Emma exclaimed, ruffling her little brother's hair.

With the fabric cut, Mr. Bennett helped drape it over the bookshelf, creating a surprisingly tree-like shape. Jack carefully stacked his wooden blocks at the base, forming a perfect trunk.

"It's starting to look like a tree," Mrs. Bennett said, smiling. "But what about decorations?"

Emma bit her lip, thinking hard. "We'll have to get creative. Everyone, let's gather anything shiny or colorful we can find!"

The family scattered throughout the house, searching for makeshift ornaments. They reconvened a few minutes later, arms full of potential decorations.

Jack had brought his collection of colorful marbles and a string of clip-on bow ties. Mr. Bennett contributed some old CDs that caught the light beautifully. Mrs. Bennett arrived with a handful of costume jewelry and some bright ribbons from her gift-wrapping stash.

Emma had the clever idea of using clothespins to attach everything to their fabric tree. Soon, their creation was adorned with glittering jewels, shimmering discs, and colorful bows.

For a garland, they strung together paper clips and draped them across the "branches." Emma even figured out how to hang the marbles by wrapping them in small squares of fabric and tying them with ribbon.

As they worked, the living room filled with laughter and Christmas music. Even though it wasn't the tree they had originally planned, there was something special about creating it together.

"Wait!" Jack suddenly exclaimed. "We forgot the star!"

The family paused, realizing they had no star for the top of their unique tree. They looked around the room, searching for inspiration.

That's when Emma spotted her old science fair project in the corner – a model of the solar system. "I have an idea," she said, grabbing the golden-painted Styrofoam ball that represented the sun.

With some clever maneuvering and a bit of tape, they secured the "sun" to the top of their bookshelf tree. It wasn't a traditional star, but it shone just as brightly.

Stepping back, the Bennetts admired their handiwork. Their tree was far from perfect – a bit lopsided, with unusual ornaments and a sun instead of a star – but to them, it was beautiful.

"You know," Mr. Bennett said, putting his arms around his family, "I think this might be the best Christmas tree we've ever had."

Mrs. Bennett nodded, her eyes twinkling. "It certainly tells a story, doesn't it?"

As the clock struck midnight, signaling the start of Christmas Day, the Bennetts gathered around their one-of-a-kind tree, feeling the true spirit of the season – love, togetherness, and the magic of creating something special as a family.

As Christmas morning dawned, the Bennett family awoke to the soft glow of their unique tree. The sunlight streaming through the window made the CDs shimmer and the costume jewelry sparkle, casting playful patterns across the living room walls.

Jack was the first to rush downstairs, his eyes wide with wonder. "It's even more beautiful in the morning light!" he exclaimed.

The rest of the family soon joined him, gathering around their creation. They spent a moment in quiet appreciation before diving into their Christmas morning traditions.

As they opened gifts, shared laughter, and enjoyed their time together, the homemade tree stood as a testament to their creativity and family bond. Each unusual ornament seemed to hold a story – Jack's marbles reminded them of family game nights, while Mrs. Bennett's ribbons brought back memories of past Christmases.

Later that day, as neighbors and friends dropped by to exchange holiday wishes, the Bennetts found themselves proudly explaining their unconventional tree.

"We forgot to get a tree," Emma would begin, "so we made one instead!"

To their surprise, their visitors were enchanted by the story and the tree itself. Many commented on how special and meaningful it was, far beyond any store-bought decoration.

"You've started quite a lovely tradition," their neighbor, Mrs. Thompson, remarked. "It's a wonderful reminder of what Christmas is truly about – family, creativity, and making the best of any situation."

Her words struck a chord with the Bennetts. What had started as a potential disaster had turned into something far more valuable than they could have imagined.

That evening, as they sat around their tree enjoying hot cocoa, Mr. Bennett raised an important question. "So, what do you all think? Should we go back to a regular tree next year?"

There was a moment of silence as everyone considered. Then, one by one, they all shook their heads.

"I think," Mrs. Bennett said slowly, "that we might have stumbled upon a new family tradition."

Emma nodded enthusiastically. "Yeah! We could do this every year, but make it different each time. We could challenge ourselves to use new materials or have a theme!"

"Like a space theme!" Jack chimed in, pointing at the sun-star topper. "Or we could make it look like a snowman next year!"

As they continued to brainstorm ideas for future trees, the Bennetts realized that their forgetfulness had led to something truly special. They had discovered that Christmas magic didn't come from perfect decorations or strictly followed traditions, but from the love, laughter, and togetherness they shared as a family.

Years later, long after Emma and Jack had grown up and started families of their own, the story of the Last-Minute Christmas Tree remained a cherished part of the Bennett family lore. And every year, no matter where they were, each member of the family would create their own unique tree, carrying on the tradition that had begun on that forgotten Christmas Eve.

In Pine Valley, the Bennetts became known as the family with the ever-changing Christmas tree, and their home was always a must-visit during the holiday season. People would come from all around to see what creative masterpiece they had come up with each year.

But more importantly, the Bennetts had learned a precious lesson about the true spirit of Christmas – that with love, creativity, and togetherness, any challenge could be turned into a beautiful memory.

So, dear children, remember the story of the Bennett family's Last-Minute Christmas Tree. It teaches us that sometimes the most magical Christmas moments come from unexpected places. With a little creativity and a lot of love, you can create your own special traditions that will warm your heart for years to come.

Chapter 14:
The Toy That Wouldn't Give Up

In a bustling toy workshop on the outskirts of Tinsel Town, where elves scurried about with paint brushes and screwdrivers, there lived a little toy robot named Rusty. Rusty wasn't the shiniest robot on the shelf, nor was he the most advanced. His gears sometimes squeaked, and his left arm had a tendency to stick, but what Rusty lacked in perfection, he made up for in heart.

Every day, Rusty watched as shiny new toys rolled off the assembly line, destined for the homes of excited children. He longed to join them, to be the cherished companion of a child who would love him despite his flaws.

As Christmas approached, the workshop buzzed with increased activity. Toys were being polished, packaged, and prepared for delivery. Rusty's hopes soared. Surely, this would be his year!

But then, disaster struck. During a final inspection, Rusty's left arm jammed completely. No matter how hard the elf technicians tried, they couldn't get it to move.

"I'm sorry, Rusty," said Gizmo, the head elf engineer, his voice heavy with regret. "We can't send you out like this. You'll have to stay behind this Christmas."

Rusty's circuits felt like they might short out from disappointment. But deep in his mechanical heart, a spark of determination flickered to life. He wouldn't give up. He couldn't! There had to be a way to fix himself in time for Christmas.

That night, after all the elves had gone home, Rusty climbed down from his shelf. His stuck arm made it difficult, but he was determined. He waddled over to the tool bench, his gears whirring with effort.

"Okay, Rusty," he said to himself, his voice box crackling with static. "Time to fix yourself!"

He tried oiling his joints, but his stubborn arm wouldn't budge. He attempted to tighten his screws, but he couldn't reach them all with just one working arm. Hours passed, and still, Rusty couldn't fix himself.

As dawn broke, Rusty heard the elves returning. Quickly, he scrambled back to his shelf, oil-stained and disheartened, but not defeated.

Day after day, night after night, Rusty continued his secret repair attempts. He studied the other robots, watching how their arms moved. He listened to the elves discuss mechanics, picking up tips and tricks. But despite all his efforts, his arm remained stubbornly stuck.

Christmas Eve arrived, and the workshop was in a frenzy of last-minute preparations. Rusty watched sadly as the last batch of toys was packed up for delivery. Just as he was about to give up hope, he heard a commotion.

"Oh no!" cried Tinsel, one of the younger elves. "The star of the Prima Ballerina doll is missing! We can't send her out like this!"

Rusty's sensors perked up. The Prima Ballerina was one of the most anticipated toys of the year. Without her star, she wouldn't be complete.

Rusty made a decision. He may not be able to fix himself, but perhaps he could help fix someone else. With great effort, he detached the small golden star that served as his power button. It wasn't easy with only one working arm, but Rusty was determined.

"Excuse me," he called out, his voice barely above a whisper. "Would this work?"

The elves turned, astonished to see Rusty holding out his star. Gizmo rushed over, gently taking the star from Rusty's outstretched hand.

"Rusty," Gizmo said, his eyes wide with surprise, "are you sure? Without this, you might not... function properly."

Rusty nodded bravely. "I'm sure. Every toy deserves a chance to make a child happy on Christmas."

The elves were deeply moved by Rusty's selfless act. Gizmo carefully attached Rusty's star to the Prima Ballerina doll, completing her outfit just in time.

As the elves prepared to leave, Gizmo turned back to Rusty. "Thank you, Rusty. You've shown us what the true spirit of Christmas is all about. Now, let's see what we can do about that arm of yours."

To Rusty's amazement, all the elves gathered around him. Each one contributed their unique skills - oiling, tightening, adjusting. They worked through the night, determined to help the little robot who had given so much.

As the first light of Christmas morning filtered through the workshop windows, Rusty felt a strange sensation. His left arm... it was moving!

"You did it!" Rusty exclaimed, waving both arms with joy. "Thank you, thank you!"

But the elves weren't finished yet. They polished Rusty until he shone, and Gizmo even fashioned a new power button for him - a beautiful silver snowflake that glittered in the light.

"Now," said Gizmo with a smile, "I think it's time for you to bring some Christmas joy to a special child."

Before Rusty could process what was happening, he found himself carefully wrapped and placed in Santa's sleigh, just as the first rays of Christmas sun peeked over the horizon.

Rusty's journey ended at a small house on the outskirts of a quiet town. As Santa gently placed him under the tree, Rusty felt a mix of excitement and nervousness. What if the child didn't like him?

He didn't have long to worry. Soon, the pitter-patter of small feet announced the arrival of a little boy named Tommy. Tommy's eyes lit up when he saw Rusty.

"A robot!" he exclaimed, carefully lifting Rusty from under the tree. "And look, he has a snowflake button, just like the snowflakes outside!"

As Tommy played with him, Rusty realized something wonderful. His arm might not work perfectly, and his gears might still squeak a bit, but to Tommy, he was perfect just the way he was.

Years passed, and while other toys came and went, Rusty remained Tommy's faithful companion. His paint may have chipped, and his gears may have grown a bit rustier, but the love between the boy and his robot only grew stronger.

And every Christmas, as Tommy placed Rusty in a place of honor on the mantelpiece, the little robot's snowflake power button would shimmer in the twinkling lights. It served as a reminder of the Christmas when a small, imperfect toy's big heart and determination brought joy not just to one child, but to an entire workshop of elves.

So, little ones, remember Rusty's story. It teaches us that it's not about being perfect, but about having the heart to keep trying and the willingness to help others. Sometimes, the greatest gifts come in unexpected packages, and the truest beauty lies in our imperfections and the love we share.

Chapter 15:
The Night the Christmas Lights Danced

In the quiet town of Merry Grove, where every house twinkled with festive lights and every yard boasted at least one inflatable Santa, there lived a little girl named Lucy. Lucy loved everything about Christmas, but most of all, she loved the lights. Every night in December, she would press her nose against her bedroom window, marveling at the colorful displays that transformed her neighborhood into a winter wonderland.

Lucy had a secret, though. A secret she had never told anyone, not even her parents. You see, Lucy believed that on Christmas Eve, when the clock struck midnight, the Christmas lights came to life and danced.

Of course, nobody believed her. Her older brother, Tom, would roll his eyes and say, "Lucy, lights don't dance. They're just bulbs and wires." Even her best friend, Emma, would giggle and say, "You have such a big imagination, Lucy!"

But Lucy knew what she had seen. Every Christmas Eve, she would stay awake, fighting off sleep, until the magical moment arrived. And every year, just as the town clock chimed midnight, she would see the lights begin to twinkle and sway in a way that had nothing to do with the winter wind.

This year, Lucy was determined to prove she wasn't imagining things. She had a plan.

On Christmas Eve, after her parents tucked her in and wished her sweet dreams, Lucy quietly slipped out of bed. She put on her warmest pajamas, her fluffy reindeer slippers, and her coziest robe. Then, she tiptoed downstairs and out the back door into the crisp night air.

The night was clear and cold, stars twinkling overhead like distant Christmas lights. Lucy's breath came out in little puffs of steam as she made her way to the old treehouse in the backyard. From there, she would have a perfect view of the entire neighborhood.

As she climbed the wooden ladder, Lucy's heart raced with excitement. This year, she would see everything clearly. This year, she would have proof!

Settled into the treehouse with her favorite blanket wrapped around her shoulders, Lucy waited. The town was quiet, most people fast asleep in their beds, dreaming of the gifts morning would bring. But Lucy's eyes were wide open, darting from house to house, watching the steady glow of countless Christmas lights.

The town clock began to chime. Lucy held her breath. One... two... three... The chimes seemed to go on forever. Finally, at the twelfth chime, it happened.

At first, it was subtle. A slight flicker here, a gentle sway there. Then, as if someone had flipped a switch, every Christmas light in Merry Grove sprang to life!

Icicle lights dangling from rooftops began to sway and twirl like ballroom dancers. Strings of colorful bulbs wrapped around trees started to pulse and wave, as if moved by an invisible breeze. Even the inflatable decorations seemed to come alive, bobbing and swaying in time to an unheard melody.

Lucy's eyes grew wide with wonder. It was even more magical than she had remembered!

But the real show was just beginning. Suddenly, a strand of golden lights unhooked itself from the Johnson's house and floated through the air. It was joined by a string of red lights from the Patels' home, then blue from the Garcias'. Soon, the night sky was filled with floating, swirling strands of Christmas lights.

The lights began to form shapes in the sky. First, a giant Christmas tree, twinkling with every color imaginable. Then, a massive snowflake that seemed to sparkle with frost. The shapes shifted and changed, creating a reindeer with a glowing red nose, then Santa's sleigh, complete with eight tiny light-reindeer pulling it across the star-studded sky.

Lucy could hardly believe her eyes. She wanted to shout, to wake up the whole town so they could see this incredible sight. But she knew that would break the magic. So she sat in silent awe, watching the dance of the lights.

As the light show reached its peak, something even more extraordinary happened. The dancing lights began to drift down towards the houses, gently touching the windows of sleeping children. As each light made contact, it seemed to sprinkle a shower of golden sparks before returning to its original position.

Lucy realized she was witnessing something truly special - the lights were spreading Christmas magic to every home in Merry Grove!

Just as the town clock began to chime one o'clock, the lights gave one final, brilliant flash. Then, as quickly as it had begun, the dance was over. The lights settled back into their usual positions, glowing steadily as if nothing had happened.

Lucy sat in the treehouse for a few more minutes, her heart full of joy and wonder. She knew she had seen something magical, something that most people would never believe. But that was okay. Some kinds of magic, she realized, were meant to be kept as special secrets.

As she climbed down from the treehouse and made her way back to her warm bed, Lucy noticed something glittering on her robe. She looked closer and gasped. There, clinging to the fuzzy fabric, were tiny specks of golden light - magical dust from the dancing Christmas lights!

The next morning, Lucy woke up to the excited shouts of her brother. "Lucy! Lucy! Wake up! It's Christmas!"

As she rubbed the sleep from her eyes, Lucy remembered the magical dance she had witnessed. Had it all been a dream? But then she saw her robe, still sparkling with tiny golden specks, and she smiled. It had been real.

Downstairs, her family marveled at the presents under the tree. But Lucy's mother noticed something strange.

"That's odd," she said, peering out the window. "I could have sworn we put the lights on the left side of the bush, but now they're on the right."

Lucy caught her brother's eye and winked. "Maybe they danced in the night," she said with a grin.

Tom rolled his eyes, but Lucy noticed a flicker of curiosity in his expression. Maybe, just maybe, a little bit of Christmas magic had touched him too.

From that day on, Lucy kept the secret of the dancing lights close to her heart. Each Christmas Eve, she would watch from her window, smiling as the familiar dance began. And each Christmas morning, she would notice the little changes - a strand of lights slightly out of place, a decoration facing a different direction - small signs of the magical night that only she knew about.

As Lucy grew older, she never lost her belief in the magic of Christmas. Even when she became a grown-up with children of her own, she would smile a secret smile when her kids asked why the Christmas lights seemed to change position overnight.

"Well," she would say, her eyes twinkling with the memory of that special night, "Christmas is a magical time. And sometimes, if you believe hard enough and watch closely enough, you might just see that magic come to life."

So, little ones, the next time you see Christmas lights twinkling in the night, look closely. Who knows? You might just catch them in the middle of their secret dance, spreading Christmas magic to all who believe.

Chapter 16:
The Forgotten Ornament

High up on the top shelf of the Wilsons' attic, in a dusty old box that hadn't been opened in years, lived an ornament named Oliver. Oliver was an antique glass bauble, hand-painted with delicate snowflakes and silver stars. He had once been the pride of the family's Christmas tree, but as newer, shinier ornaments arrived over the years, Oliver found himself used less and less, until finally, he was packed away and forgotten.

Year after year, Oliver would hear the excitement below as the family brought out their Christmas decorations. He would listen to the cheerful voices and the rustle of tissue paper as other ornaments were unwrapped, but his box remained untouched.

"Maybe this year," Oliver would whisper to himself each December, but each year brought only disappointment.

Despite the loneliness, Oliver never lost his Christmas spirit. He would spend his days remembering the joy he once brought to the family and dreaming of the day he might do so again. At night, when the attic was quiet, he would softly hum the Christmas carols he remembered from years past.

This year, as the sounds of holiday preparation echoed from below, Oliver heard something different - the creak of the attic ladder.

"Mom, are you sure there aren't any more ornaments up here?" called a young voice. "We need more for the tree!"

Oliver's glass heart seemed to skip a beat. Could it be? After all these years?

A moment later, a flashlight beam cut through the darkness, illuminating the dusty shelves. Oliver wanted to shout, to wave, to do anything to draw attention to his box, but of course, he couldn't move. He was, after all, just an ornament.

The light passed over him once, twice, and Oliver felt his hopes beginning to fade. But then...

"Hey, what's this?" The young voice belonged to Emma, the Wilsons' ten-year-old daughter. She reached up and carefully took down Oliver's box. "Mom! I found something!"

As Emma carried the box downstairs, Oliver could hardly contain his excitement. After so long in the dark, quiet attic, the lights and sounds of the living room were almost overwhelming.

"Oh my," Mrs. Wilson gasped as Emma opened the box. "I had completely forgotten about these! They were your great-grandmother's ornaments."

Gentle hands lifted Oliver from his tissue paper nest. As the dust was carefully brushed away, his painted snowflakes and stars gleamed in the light.

"It's beautiful," Emma breathed, turning Oliver gently to admire every angle.

"Indeed it is," Mr. Wilson agreed. "You know, these ornaments have a special story. Your great-grandmother used to tell us that each one held memories of past Christmases. She said if you listened closely on Christmas Eve, you could hear the ornaments sharing their stories."

Emma's eyes widened with wonder. "Really? Can we hang them on the tree?"

And so, for the first time in many years, Oliver found himself nestled among the branches of the Christmas tree. The lights twinkled around him, and the scent of pine filled the air. Oliver had never felt happier.

That night, as the house grew quiet and the only light came from the glowing tree, something magical happened. Oliver found he could speak!

"Hello, everyone," he said softly. "It's so wonderful to be back on the tree."

The other ornaments were startled at first, but soon they were all chattering excitedly.

"Welcome back!" chirped a cheerful red ball. "I'm Ruby. What's your name?"

"I'm Oliver," he replied. "It's nice to meet you all."

A glittery snowflake twirled on her thread. "Where have you been all this time, Oliver? We've never seen you before."

And so, Oliver began to tell his story. He spoke of Christmases long past, of the first Wilson family Christmas when he was new, of the year the twins were born and how the parents were too tired to put up more than a few ornaments, of the Christmas when the family's old dog accidentally knocked over the tree.

The other ornaments listened in awe. Even the newest, fanciest baubles were captivated by Oliver's tales.

"Wow," said a shiny blue icicle. "You've seen so much!"

Oliver smiled (as much as an ornament can smile). "Every ornament has a story," he said. "What are yours?"

For the rest of the night, the tree was alive with whispered stories. Each ornament, from the oldest to the newest, shared their memories. There were tales of joyous Christmases, of quiet ones, of years when money was tight and years of plenty. Through it all ran a common thread - the love of the Wilson family and the magic of the holiday season.

As dawn broke on Christmas morning, the ornaments fell silent once more. But there was a new sense of camaraderie among them, a shared history that made them all feel more special.

Emma was the first one down the stairs that morning. As she approached the tree, she could have sworn she heard the faintest whisper of voices. She leaned in close to Oliver, remembering what her father had said about the ornaments telling stories.

For a moment, she thought she heard a gentle voice say, "Merry Christmas, Emma." But then she shook her head, convincing herself it was just her imagination.

As she stepped back, though, Emma noticed something extraordinary. All the ornaments on the tree seemed to be glowing with a warm, gentle light that had nothing to do with the tree's electric lights. It was as if each one was shining with the joy of the stories and memories it held.

From that year on, Oliver was always given a place of honor on the Wilson family Christmas tree. Emma made sure of it, carefully unpacking him first each year. And though she grew older and eventually had a family of her own, she never forgot the magic she felt that Christmas morning.

Many years later, Emma sat with her own daughter, carefully unwrapping Oliver to place him on their tree.

"You know," she said, her eyes twinkling, "this ornament has a very special story. Some say that on Christmas Eve, if you listen very closely, you can hear it sharing memories of Christmases past."

Her daughter's eyes widened with wonder, just as Emma's had so many years ago. And as they hung Oliver on the tree, Emma could have sworn she heard a faint, familiar voice say, "Thank you for remembering."

So, little ones, remember that every ornament, no matter how old or new, holds a special kind of magic. They're more than just decorations - they're keepers of memories, holders of stories, and reminders of the enduring spirit of Christmas. So this year, as you decorate your tree, take a moment to listen. You never know what stories you might hear.

Chapter 17:
Mrs. Claus's Secret Recipe

At the North Pole, where the Northern Lights danced in the sky and the snow sparkled like diamond dust, there was a cozy kitchen that always smelled of cinnamon and chocolate. This was Mrs. Claus's domain, and it was here that she created her famous hot chocolate - a brew so delicious that it was said to warm not just the body, but the soul.

Every Christmas Eve, as Santa prepared for his globe-trotting journey, Mrs. Claus would brew a special batch of her hot chocolate. This magical concoction kept Santa warm on his long night of deliveries and gave him the energy to visit every child in the world.

But this year was different. As Mrs. Claus entered her kitchen on the morning of Christmas Eve, she found something was terribly wrong.

"Oh, dear!" she exclaimed, her usual cheery voice filled with dismay. "The recipe! It's gone!"

The elves, who had been busily preparing Christmas treats, stopped in their tracks. Jingle, the head kitchen elf, rushed to Mrs. Claus's side.

"Gone, Mrs. Claus? But how can that be?" he asked, his pointy ears twitching with concern.

Mrs. Claus shook her head, bewildered. "I don't know, Jingle. I always keep it right here in this special candy cane tin. But it's empty!"

Word of the missing recipe spread through Santa's workshop like wildfire. Elves abandoned their toy-making stations to join the search. Even the reindeer, sensing the urgency, began sniffing around for clues.

Santa himself, in the midst of checking his list for the second time, hurried to the kitchen. "Now, now," he said, trying to calm everyone down. "I'm sure it'll turn up. Have you checked under the cookie jars?"

But as the hours ticked by and every nook and cranny of the North Pole had been searched, the recipe was still nowhere to be found. Mrs. Claus wrung her hands in worry.

"Oh, Santa," she fretted, "what are we going to do? You can't make your journey without the hot chocolate. You'll freeze out there!"

Santa patted her hand comfortingly, though his brow was furrowed with concern. "Don't worry, my dear. We'll think of something."

Just then, Pepper, the youngest elf in the kitchen, piped up. "Mrs. Claus," she said timidly, "couldn't you just make the hot chocolate from memory? You've been making it for centuries, after all."

Mrs. Claus smiled kindly at Pepper. "Oh, sweetie, I wish I could. But the recipe is so complex, with so many secret ingredients, that even I can't remember it all. That's why I wrote it down in the first place."

As the situation grew more desperate, Jingle had an idea. "What if," he suggested, his eyes brightening, "we all worked together to recreate the recipe? We may not remember all of it, but maybe between all of us, we can piece it together!"

Mrs. Claus clapped her hands in delight. "Jingle, that's brilliant! Let's give it a try."

And so began The Great Hot Chocolate Experiment. Elves from every department joined in, each contributing what they remembered about Mrs. Claus's famous brew.

"I remember it had a hint of peppermint," said Holly from the gift-wrapping department.

"And a dash of cinnamon," added Twinkle from the star-polishing team.

"Don't forget the secret blend of cocoas," chimed in Boots, who usually worked in the reindeer stables but had a surprising knowledge of fine chocolates.

Mrs. Claus directed the efforts, her expert palate guiding the elves as they mixed and taste-tested batch after batch. Some attempts were too sweet, others not sweet enough. One batch turned an alarming shade of green (thanks to an overzealous addition of mint), while another was so thick you could stand a candy cane up in it.

As the clock ticked closer to Santa's departure time, tension in the kitchen grew. Would they be able to recreate the magic in time?

Just as they were about to test their fifteenth batch, there was a commotion at the kitchen door. In burst Rudolph, his red nose glowing brightly, pulling something in his mouth. It was the candy cane tin!

"Rudolph!" Santa exclaimed. "Where did you find that?"

The red-nosed reindeer dropped the tin and shuffled his hooves sheepishly. As it turned out, he had "borrowed" the tin the night before, enticed by the lingering smell of peppermint. He had planned to return it before anyone noticed, but had fallen asleep in the barn with it next to him.

There was a moment of stunned silence, then the kitchen erupted in cheers and laughter. Mrs. Claus scooped up the tin, quickly reviewing her recipe.

"Well, I'll be a sugar plum fairy," she chuckled. "It looks like our experiment wasn't too far off after all!"

With the original recipe in hand, Mrs. Claus quickly whipped up a batch of her famous hot chocolate. The rich, sweet aroma filled the air, bringing smiles to every face.

Santa took a sip and let out a contented sigh. "Perfect as always, my dear," he said, giving Mrs. Claus a kiss on the cheek. "I don't know what I'd do without you – or your hot chocolate!"

As Santa took off into the night sky, thermos of hot chocolate securely packed, Mrs. Claus turned to the tired but happy group of elves.

"You know," she said thoughtfully, "I think it's time this recipe was shared. After all, you've all proven yourselves to be excellent hot chocolate makers."

And so, Mrs. Claus spent the rest of the night teaching the elves the intricacies of her secret recipe. By the time Santa returned, the North Pole had a whole team of hot chocolate experts.

From that Christmas on, Mrs. Claus's hot chocolate became not just a secret recipe, but a beloved tradition shared by all at the North Pole. Elves would gather in the kitchen on cold nights, each adding their own special touch to the brew. Some added extra marshmallows, others a sprinkle of coconut. But at the heart of every cup was Mrs. Claus's original recipe – a perfect blend of sweetness, warmth, and Christmas magic.

And Rudolph? Well, he was given his very own candy cane tin, filled with peppermint treats. After all, his "borrowing" had led to a wonderful new North Pole tradition.

So, little ones, remember that sometimes the most magical recipes aren't just about the ingredients, but about the love and teamwork that goes into making them. And who knows? Maybe one day, if you listen to the winter wind just right, you might catch a whiff of Mrs. Claus's famous hot chocolate, warming hearts all around the world.

Chapter 18:
The Christmas Tree Forest

Deep in the heart of the Evergreen Valley, where snow blanketed the ground year-round and the air always smelled of pine, there grew a very special forest. This was no ordinary woodland, but the Christmas Tree Forest, where every tree dreamed of one day becoming the centerpiece of a family's holiday celebration.

Among these trees was a young pine named Pip. Pip wasn't the tallest tree in the forest, nor was he the fullest. His branches were a bit crooked, and his needles stuck out at odd angles. But what Pip lacked in perfect appearance, he made up for in heart and determination.

Every year, as the holiday season approached, Pip would stretch his branches as high as he could, hoping to catch the eye of the tree farmer, Old Jack. Old Jack was responsible for choosing which trees would be cut down and sent to homes for Christmas.

"This year," Pip would whisper to himself, "this year will be my turn."

The older trees around Pip would rustle their needles indulgently. "Oh, Pip," they'd say, "you're still too small. Maybe in a few years."

But Pip refused to be discouraged. He spent his days dreaming of the moment when he would be chosen, imagining the joy he would bring to a family's home. At night, he would listen to the wind carrying stories of Christmases past, told by the ancient pines at the edge of the forest.

As another Christmas season arrived, Pip was more determined than ever. He had grown a few inches over the past year and had worked hard to make his needles as green and fragrant as possible.

The day Old Jack came to select the trees, Pip stood as tall and straight as he could. He watched with a mixture of excitement and envy as tree after tree was chosen and carefully cut down.

Just when Pip thought all hope was lost, he heard a small voice.

"Daddy, what about this one?"

Pip's branches quivered with anticipation as a little girl with bright eyes and a red wool hat pointed directly at him. Old Jack knelt down beside the girl, examining Pip closely.

"Well, Sarah," Old Jack said gently, "this tree is a bit small and crooked. Are you sure you don't want a bigger one?"

Sarah shook her head firmly. "No, Daddy. This one's perfect. It's just my size!"

Old Jack chuckled and nodded. "Alright then, if you're sure."

Pip could hardly believe it. He was being chosen! As Old Jack's saw began to cut through his trunk, Pip felt a moment of fear. But then he remembered all his dreams of bringing joy to a family, and he stood proud and tall.

The journey to Sarah's home was a whirlwind of new experiences for Pip. He was bundled up and tied to the top of a car, watching in wonder as the landscape changed from snowy forest to busy town. When they arrived at a small, cozy-looking house, Pip was carried inside and placed in a stand in the corner of a warm living room.

Sarah and her family spent the evening decorating Pip with twinkling lights, shiny ornaments, and strings of popcorn. Pip had never felt so beautiful or important in his life.

As the days passed, Pip watched the family's Christmas preparations with delight. He saw cookies being baked, presents being wrapped, and heard carols being sung. Each night, Sarah would sit by Pip and tell him about her day at school or her excitement for Christmas morning.

On Christmas Eve, as the family gathered around Pip to place the final presents under his branches, he heard Sarah's mother say something that made his pine needles tingle with joy.

"You know," she said, smiling at Sarah, "I think this is the most perfect Christmas tree we've ever had. It has so much character!"

Sarah beamed with pride, gently touching one of Pip's branches. "I knew he was special from the moment I saw him," she said.

That night, as the house grew quiet and the only light came from Pip's twinkling decorations, something magical happened. Pip felt a warmth spreading through his branches, and suddenly, he could speak!

"Thank you," he whispered to the sleeping house. "Thank you for choosing me and making my dreams come true."

To Pip's amazement, the other decorations on his branches began to stir.

"Well, well," said a glittery star ornament. "Looks like we have a talking tree this year!"

"Welcome to the family," chirped a little bird ornament. "We've been part of their Christmases for years."

Throughout the night, the ornaments shared stories with Pip about past Christmases and the joy they'd brought to the family. Pip listened in wonder, feeling more and more a part of this special tradition.

As dawn broke on Christmas morning, Pip heard the excited footsteps of Sarah running down the stairs. The living room soon filled with laughter and excitement as presents were opened and stockings emptied.

Pip stood tall and proud, his branches holding the family's gifts and his lights adding to the warm glow of the room. He knew that this was what he had been growing for all those years in the forest – this moment of pure Christmas joy.

After the excitement of gift-opening had passed, Sarah came and sat by Pip once more. "Merry Christmas, little tree," she said softly, gently touching his needles. "You've made this the best Christmas ever."

Pip's heart swelled with happiness. He may not have been the biggest or the most perfectly shaped tree in the forest, but here, in this home, he was absolutely perfect.

As the days passed and Christmas came to an end, Pip began to worry about what would happen to him. Would he be thrown out and forgotten? But Sarah's family had other plans.

Instead of discarding Pip, they carefully removed his decorations and carried him out to the backyard. There, they planted him in a special spot where he could continue to grow.

"Now we can see you all year round," Sarah explained, patting the soil around Pip's roots. "And maybe next year, we can decorate you right here in the yard!"

Pip's branches quivered with joy. Not only had he fulfilled his dream of being a Christmas tree, but now he had a permanent home with a family who loved him.

As the years passed, Pip grew taller and stronger. Each Christmas, Sarah and her family would decorate him with outdoor lights and ornaments, making him the centerpiece of their holiday yard display. And each year, Pip would remember his journey from the Christmas Tree Forest and the magic of that first Christmas in Sarah's home.

Sometimes, on quiet winter nights, Pip would whisper his story to the wind, hoping it would carry back to the Christmas Tree Forest. He wanted all the little trees there to know that no matter their size or shape, they too could make Christmas dreams come true.

So, little ones, the next time you see a Christmas tree, remember Pip's story. Every tree, no matter how small or crooked, has the potential to bring joy and magic to someone's holiday. It's not about being perfect – it's about being perfectly loved.

Chapter 19:
The Snowman's Warm Heart

In a small town nestled at the foot of snow-capped mountains, where icicles hung from every rooftop and the air sparkled with frost, there lived a most unusual snowman. His name was Frosty (no relation to the famous one), and he had a secret that set him apart from every other snowman in the world: Frosty had a warm heart.

Now, you might wonder how a snowman could have a warm heart. Wouldn't he melt? Well, Frosty often wondered the same thing. You see, he hadn't always been this way.

Frosty had been built by the children of Evergreen Lane on a crisp December morning. They had rolled three perfect snowballs for his body, found two lumps of coal for his eyes, and a carrot for his nose. But when it came time for his heart, little Sophie, the youngest of the children, had an idea.

"Let's give him a special heart," she said, her eyes twinkling with excitement. From her pocket, she pulled out a small, heart-shaped stone she had found in the summer. It was smooth and red, warm from being in her pocket all morning.

As Sophie placed the stone in the center of Frosty's chest, something magical happened. A warm glow spread through his snowy body, and Frosty felt himself come to life!

At first, Frosty was overjoyed. He could move! He could think! He could even speak (though only the children seemed to hear him). But as night fell and the children went home, Frosty began to worry. What if his warm heart made him melt?

But to Frosty's surprise, he didn't melt. The warm heart seemed to exist in perfect balance with his snowy exterior. However, it did give him a unique ability – Frosty could feel emotions just like humans did.

As the days passed, Frosty watched the comings and goings on Evergreen Lane. He saw families decorating their homes for Christmas, smelled the aroma of freshly baked cookies wafting from open windows, and heard the cheerful sounds of carols being sung.

But Frosty also noticed things that made his warm heart ache. He saw old Mr. Johnson struggling to shovel his driveway, his arthritic hands shaking with cold. He watched as little Timmy from next door pressed his nose against the toy store window, longing for a train set his family couldn't afford. And he noticed Mrs. Baker, a widow, sitting alone by her window night after night, a sad expression on her face.

Frosty wished he could help, but what could a snowman do?

Then, on Christmas Eve, something wonderful happened. As Frosty stood in his usual spot, watching the gently falling snow, he felt a strange tingling in his stick arms. To his amazement, he could move them! Not just a little, but fully and freely.

Hardly daring to believe it, Frosty took a tentative step forward. His snow legs held! Overcome with excitement, Frosty began to walk down Evergreen Lane, leaving a trail of snowy footprints behind him.

As he passed Mr. Johnson's house, Frosty had an idea. He picked up the shovel leaning against the porch and began to clear the driveway. His snowy body didn't tire, and soon the entire driveway was clear.

Next, Frosty waddled to the toy store. The owner had forgotten to lock the door in his haste to get home for Christmas Eve dinner. Frosty slipped inside and, using the money little Sophie had accidentally left in the pocket of his scarf (she had been saving it for hot chocolate), he bought the train set Timmy had been admiring. He left it on Timmy's doorstep with a note signed "From Santa."

Finally, Frosty made his way to Mrs. Baker's house. He knew he couldn't take away her loneliness, but maybe he could bring her a little Christmas cheer. Using twigs from a nearby bush, he fashioned a small Christmas tree. He decorated it with icicles and berries, and topped it with a star made from his own carrot nose. He left this on Mrs. Baker's porch, again with a note from "Santa."

As dawn broke on Christmas morning, Frosty hurried back to his spot on Evergreen Lane. Just as the sun peeked over the horizon, he felt the magic fading. His stick arms grew stiff once more, and his snow legs froze in place. But Frosty didn't mind. His warm heart glowed with happiness, knowing he had made a difference.

The residents of Evergreen Lane were amazed by the mysterious events of Christmas Eve. Mr. Johnson was touched by the kindness of his "secret shoveler." Timmy was overjoyed with his surprise gift, and Mrs. Baker's heart was warmed by the thoughtful little tree.

As the children came out to play in the snow, they gathered around Frosty, telling him all about the Christmas magic that had happened overnight. If snowmen could smile, Frosty would have been beaming.

Little Sophie noticed something different about Frosty. "Look!" she exclaimed. "Frosty's heart is glowing!"

Indeed, a warm red glow could be seen emanating from Frosty's chest, right where his heart-shaped stone sat.

From that day on, the residents of Evergreen Lane took special care of Frosty. When the weather grew warm, they built a special refrigerated gazebo to keep him cool. They decorated him for every holiday and told him all their stories.

And every Christmas Eve, if you watched very closely, you might see a snowman waddling down Evergreen Lane, leaving a trail of kindness in his wake. For Frosty had learned that the true magic of his warm heart wasn't just that it kept him alive – it was that it gave him the power to bring joy to others.

Years passed, and the children of Evergreen Lane grew up. But they never forgot Frosty. They brought their own children to visit him, telling them the story of the snowman with the warm heart who brought Christmas magic to their little street.

And Frosty, with his coal-black eyes twinkling and his warm heart glowing, listened to every story and cherished every visit. He knew that as long as there was love and kindness in the world, his warm heart would never melt.

So, little ones, remember Frosty's story. It teaches us that the warmest hearts can be found in the coldest of places, and that even the smallest acts of kindness can bring the greatest joy. This Christmas, may your hearts be as warm as Frosty's, full of love and the desire to help others.

Chapter 20:
The Elf Exchange Program

In Santa's workshop at the North Pole, where the air always smelled of peppermint and sawdust, there lived an elf named Tinsel. Tinsel was known for three things: her knack for wrapping presents, her curly green shoes, and her insatiable curiosity about the human world.

While other elves were content to focus on toy-making and cookie-baking, Tinsel would often gaze out the frost-covered windows, wondering what life was like beyond the snowy expanse of the North Pole. She'd pepper returning reindeer with questions about the children they'd seen and the homes they'd visited.

One day, as Tinsel was putting the finishing touches on a particularly tricky bow, she overheard Santa talking to Mrs. Claus.

"My dear," Santa said, his brow furrowed with concern, "I'm worried. It seems fewer children truly believe in the magic of Christmas these days. They're growing up so fast."

Mrs. Claus patted his hand comfortingly. "Perhaps what we need is a fresh perspective," she suggested. "A way to see Christmas through a child's eyes again."

Tinsel's pointy ears perked up. An idea was forming in her mind, as bright and shiny as a new Christmas bauble. She took a deep breath and approached Santa.

"Excuse me, Santa," Tinsel said, her voice quivering with excitement. "I couldn't help overhearing, and I have an idea. What if we started an Elf Exchange Program?"

Santa's bushy eyebrows rose in surprise. "An Elf Exchange Program? What do you mean, Tinsel?"

"Well," Tinsel explained, her words tumbling out in a rush, "what if an elf could swap places with a child for a day? The elf could learn about the human world, and the child could experience the magic of the North Pole firsthand!"

Santa stroked his beard thoughtfully. "That's quite an idea, Tinsel. But it would be very complicated. And potentially dangerous if our secret got out."

"Oh, but Santa," Tinsel pleaded, "think of how much we could learn! And we could use Christmas magic to keep everything safe and secret."

After much discussion and planning, Santa finally agreed to a trial run of the Elf Exchange Program. And who better to be the first elf participant than Tinsel herself?

The lucky child chosen for the exchange was a 10-year-old girl named Lucy, who lived in a small town called Evergreen. Lucy had been writing to Santa for years, always including a P.S. that said, "I'd love to visit your workshop someday!"

On the chosen day, Tinsel could hardly contain her excitement. She put on her best green and red outfit, polished her curly shoes until they shone, and tucked a small notebook into her pocket to record her observations.

With a wave of his hand, Santa cast the exchange spell. In a shower of sparkly snow, Tinsel found herself standing in Lucy's bedroom, while Lucy appeared in the North Pole workshop, her eyes wide with wonder.

Tinsel looked around the room in awe. Everything seemed so big! She ran her hands over the soft bedspread, marveled at the colorful posters on the walls, and giggled at her reflection in the mirror - she looked just like a human child now!

Just then, Lucy's mother called from downstairs. "Lucy! Time for school!"

School! Tinsel had always wondered about human schools. She found Lucy's backpack, stuffed with books and pencils, and made her way downstairs.

The day that followed was a whirlwind of new experiences for Tinsel. She rode on a yellow school bus, sat in classes where she learned about math and history, and played games at recess that didn't involve wrapping presents or candy cane races.

At lunch, Tinsel sat with Lucy's friends, carefully watching how they interacted. She was fascinated by their conversations about movies, video games, and family traditions.

"So, Lucy," one friend asked, "do you still believe in Santa?"

Tinsel nearly choked on her milk. "Of course!" she exclaimed, then quickly added, "I mean, don't you?"

The friends exchanged glances. "Well," another girl said hesitantly, "my older sister says Santa isn't real. That it's just parents buying the presents."

Tinsel felt a pang in her heart. No wonder Santa was worried about children losing their belief in Christmas magic. But how could she convince them without giving away her secret?

After school, Tinsel experienced more wonders of the human world. She watched TV, played video games with Lucy's little brother, and helped Lucy's mom prepare dinner. Each new discovery filled her with excitement and gave her ideas for new toys and games they could make at the North Pole.

As bedtime approached, Tinsel realized her day in the human world was almost over. She felt a mixture of sadness and excitement - sad to leave this fascinating world behind, but eager to share everything she'd learned.

Meanwhile, at the North Pole, Lucy was having the time of her life. She had helped make toys, decorate cookies with Mrs. Claus, and even fed the reindeer. Every moment confirmed her belief in the magic of Christmas.

As the clock struck midnight, Santa's spell activated once again. In a swirl of festive magic, Tinsel and Lucy returned to their own worlds.

Back at the North Pole, Tinsel couldn't stop talking about her adventures. She told the other elves about school and video games, about the yellow bus and the cafeteria food. But most importantly, she shared her concerns about the fading belief in Santa.

"We need to adapt," Tinsel explained. "The human world is changing, and we need to change with it. But we also need to find ways to keep the magic alive."

Inspired by Tinsel's experiences, Santa and the elves began brainstorming new ideas. They developed toys that combined traditional craftsmanship with modern technology. They updated their Christmas magic to be compatible with smart homes. And they started a secret campaign to spread random acts of kindness throughout the year, reminding people of the Christmas spirit even in the middle of summer.

Lucy, back in her own world, found her belief in Christmas magic stronger than ever. She became known in her school as the girl who always stood up for Santa, who always had a kind word for others, and who seemed to carry a bit of Christmas joy with her all year round.

The Elf Exchange Program was deemed a huge success. Over the years, more elves and children participated, each exchange bringing new ideas and renewed Christmas spirit to both worlds.

And Tinsel? Well, she became the head of North Pole Public Relations, using her knowledge of the human world to help Santa and the elves stay connected with the changing times while keeping the timeless magic of Christmas alive.

Every Christmas Eve, as Santa prepared for his flight, he would wink at Tinsel and say, "Remember, it was your curiosity that helped save the spirit of Christmas. Never stop wondering, Tinsel."

And Tinsel would smile, her heart full of joy, knowing that somewhere out there, children like Lucy were gazing at the sky, believing with all their hearts in the magic of Santa and his elves.

So, little ones, remember Tinsel's story. It teaches us that curiosity and open-mindedness can bridge any gap, even the one between our world and the magical realm of Santa. Keep your hearts open to wonder, and you might just find a bit of North Pole magic in your own backyard.

Chapter 21:
The Christmas Stocking that Wouldn't Stop Growing

In a cozy little house at the end of Mistletoe Lane lived a young girl named Lily. Lily loved everything about Christmas - the twinkling lights, the smell of gingerbread, and especially hanging up her stocking on Christmas Eve. This year, Lily had a brand new stocking. It was bright red with white fluffy trim, and her name was embroidered in gold thread at the top.

On the night before Christmas, as Lily carefully hung her stocking by the fireplace, she whispered a wish. "I wish for the best Christmas ever, filled with lots and lots of presents!"

Little did Lily know, but her new stocking was magical. As soon as the words left her lips, the stocking gave a little twitch.

The next morning, Lily woke up extra early, excited to see what Santa had brought. But when she reached the living room, she stopped in her tracks, her eyes wide with amazement.

Her stocking had grown! It was now as tall as she was, bulging with presents of all shapes and sizes.

"Wow!" Lily exclaimed, clapping her hands with glee. She immediately began to empty the stocking, finding dolls and books, art supplies and stuffed animals. It seemed like the stocking would never empty!

Lily's parents watched in bewilderment. "Santa must have been extra generous this year," her mother said, exchanging a puzzled glance with Lily's father.

As Lily played with her new toys, she thought about her cousins who were coming over later. "I wish I had presents for them too," she said absently.

To her astonishment, the stocking twitched again and began to grow even larger. More presents appeared inside, each with a tag bearing her cousins' names.

When her cousins arrived, Lily was thrilled to have gifts to share. Their eyes lit up as they opened their unexpected presents.

"This is the best Christmas ever!" Lily's youngest cousin exclaimed.

Hearing these words, Lily felt a warm glow inside. She realized that giving gifts was just as exciting as receiving them.

As the day went on, Lily began to think about others who might not have presents on Christmas. "I wish everyone could have gifts on Christmas," she said softly.

This time, the stocking's growth was dramatic. It burst out of the fireplace, growing taller and wider until it filled half the living room. Presents of all sizes poured out, spilling across the floor.

Lily's parents were astonished. "What in the world is happening?" her father asked, staring at the enormous stocking.

Lily explained about her wishes and how the stocking seemed to be granting them. Her parents listened in amazement, then looked at each other thoughtfully.

"Lily," her mother said gently, "this is an incredible gift. But with great power comes great responsibility. What do you think we should do with all these presents?"

Lily looked around at the mountain of gifts, then at her own pile of toys. She thought about how happy she'd felt giving presents to her cousins. Suddenly, she knew exactly what to do.

"We should give them away!" she said excitedly. "To people who don't have presents on Christmas!"

Her parents smiled proudly. "That's a wonderful idea, sweetheart."

And so, the family spent the rest of Christmas Day delivering presents all over town. They brought gifts to the children's hospital, to the homeless shelter, and to elderly neighbors who lived alone. Everywhere they went, they left behind smiles and joy.

As they worked, Lily noticed something interesting. The more presents they gave away, the smaller the stocking became. By the time they had delivered the last gift, the stocking had shrunk back to its original size.

That night, as Lily got ready for bed, she felt happier than she ever had before. Her mother tucked her in and kissed her forehead.

"Lily," she said, "I'm so proud of you for sharing your magical gift with others. You've learned an important lesson about the true spirit of Christmas."

Lily nodded sleepily. "It feels good to give," she said. "I think that's the real magic."

As she drifted off to sleep, Lily had one last thought. She whispered it softly into the quiet room: "I wish for everyone to feel the joy of giving."

In the living room, the stocking gave one final twitch. But this time, instead of growing, it glowed with a warm, golden light. The magic spread out from the stocking, drifting like glittering snow throughout the town.

From that Christmas on, the town of Mistletoe Lane became known for its incredible generosity during the holiday season. People found themselves looking for ways to help others and share what they had. The spirit of giving that Lily had unleashed with her magical stocking had taken root in everyone's hearts.

Years later, when Lily had children of her own, she passed down the special stocking and its story. But now, the magic worked a little differently. Instead of growing with wishes for presents, it grew when people made wishes to help others.

Every Christmas, Lily and her family would hang the stocking and make wishes for those in need. And every year, they would watch with joy as the stocking filled up, not with toys or games, but with opportunities to spread kindness and generosity throughout their community.

The magical stocking had taught Lily, and now her whole town, the most valuable Christmas lesson of all - that the true gift of the season is not what we receive, but what we give to others.

So, little ones, remember Lily's magical stocking. It reminds us that the best wishes we can make at Christmas are not for ourselves, but for others. The greatest joy comes not from what we get, but from what we give. May your own hearts grow as big as Lily's magical stocking, filled with love and generosity for all.

Chapter 22:
The Penguin's Christmas Parade

c〔∞〕ɔ

In the icy expanse of Antarctica, where the sun never sets during Christmas and the landscape is a dazzling white as far as the eye can see, there lived a colony of Emperor penguins. Among them was a particularly curious and creative penguin named Pip.

Pip wasn't like the other penguins. While his friends were content to waddle around, fish, and huddle for warmth, Pip's mind was always buzzing with questions and ideas. He was especially fascinated by the stories that Arctic seagulls would share when they visited during their global migrations.

"Tell me again about Christmas!" Pip would beg, his eyes wide with wonder as the seagulls described twinkling lights, colorful decorations, and joyous celebrations.

The other penguins would shake their heads fondly. "Oh, Pip," they'd say, "why worry about holidays from the other side of the world? We have our own traditions here."

But Pip couldn't shake the feeling that they were missing out on something special.

One day, as Pip was waddling along the ice shelf, he stumbled upon something extraordinary - a small box, half-buried in the snow. It must have fallen from a research vessel passing by. With great effort, Pip managed to dig it out and pry it open with his beak.

Inside was a treasure trove of Christmas decorations! There were tinsel garlands, small ornaments, and even a tiny snow globe with a Christmas tree inside. But what caught Pip's eye was a book titled "Christmas Around the World."

Pip couldn't read human language, of course, but the pictures in the book fired up his imagination. He saw images of Christmas parades with floats, marching bands, and people dressed in festive costumes.

That's when Pip had his brilliant idea. "We should have our own Christmas parade!" he exclaimed to no one in particular, his voice echoing across the icy expanse.

Excited, Pip waddled as fast as his little legs could carry him back to the colony. He gathered all the penguins around and shared his vision.

"Imagine," he said, his flippers waving enthusiastically, "a parade of penguins, all dressed up and celebrating! We could have music and decorations and spread joy across the ice!"

The other penguins were skeptical at first.

"But Pip," said wise old Walter, the eldest of the colony, "we're penguins. We don't have instruments or costumes or floats."

Pip's enthusiasm didn't waver. "We don't need those exact things! We can create our own Antarctic version!"

Slowly but surely, Pip's excitement began to catch on. The younger penguins were particularly intrigued by the idea of doing something new and exciting.

And so, the preparations began. Pip assigned tasks to everyone. Some penguins collected shells and shiny pebbles to use as decorations. Others practiced synchronized swimming routines to perform in the breaks in the ice shelf.

Pip showed them how to use the tinsel he'd found, draping it over their bodies like glittering scarves. The small ornaments became festive hats when balanced carefully on their heads.

For music, they discovered that tapping their beaks on different thicknesses of ice produced various tones. A group of musically inclined penguins began to practice Christmas carols - penguin style.

As for floats, Pip had a stroke of genius. He noticed how gracefully seals could slide across the ice on their bellies. With a bit of convincing (and the promise of extra fish), a few friendly seals agreed to be their "floats," with penguins riding on their backs.

The preparations weren't without challenges. More than one penguin slipped on the tinsel, sending decorations scattering across the ice. The seal-floats took some practice to master, resulting in a few comical wipeouts. And teaching an entire colony of penguins to march in formation was no easy task.

But through it all, Pip's enthusiasm never wavered. His joy was infectious, and soon even the most skeptical penguins found themselves caught up in the excitement.

Finally, the day of the parade arrived. The Antarctic sun shone brightly in the endless blue sky, making the snow and ice sparkle like diamonds.

Pip, wearing a crown made of shiny fish bones and draped in sparkling tinsel, took his place at the front of the parade. With a clear "honk," he signaled the start of the festivities.

What followed was the most extraordinary sight Antarctica had ever seen. A long line of penguins, adorned with shells, pebbles, and tinsel, waddled in surprisingly good formation across the ice. At intervals, groups would break into synchronized swimming routines in the gaps between ice floes, splashing and diving in perfect harmony.

The "penguin band" tapped out joyful rhythms on the ice, their musicality improving with each step. Seals slid gracefully along, their penguin passengers waving cheerfully.

Word of the unusual event spread quickly through the animal kingdom. Curious seabirds circled overhead, watching in amazement. Whales breached nearby, their mighty splashes adding percussion to the penguin orchestra.

Even a group of human researchers, observing from a distance, stood in awe of the spectacle. They couldn't quite believe their eyes, and more than one wondered if the endless Antarctic day was playing tricks on their minds.

As the parade wound its way across the ice, something magical began to happen. The joy that Pip had envisioned began to spread. Penguins who had never lifted their beaks from the serious business of survival found themselves "smiling" (as much as penguins can smile). The air filled with cheerful honks and squawks - the penguin equivalent of laughter and song.

By the time the parade completed its route, circling back to where it began, the entire colony was in high spirits. Pip looked around at his fellow penguins, his heart swelling with happiness. He had done it - he had brought the spirit of Christmas to Antarctica!

As the excitement began to die down and penguins started to return to their usual routines, wise old Walter approached Pip.

"You know, Pip," he said, his eyes twinkling, "I thought this idea of yours was crazy. But I haven't seen the colony this happy in years. You've given us all a wonderful gift."

Pip beamed with pride. "Thank you, Walter. I just wanted everyone to experience a bit of Christmas magic."

From that day on, the Christmas parade became an annual tradition in Pip's penguin colony. Each year, they would add new elements, inspired by stories from migrating birds or items that washed up on their shores.

The human researchers, fascinated by this unusual behavior, began to study it. They never quite figured out how it had started, but they marveled at the positive effects it had on the penguin community. Papers were written about the "Christmas-celebrating penguins of Antarctica," making Pip's colony famous in the scientific world.

As for Pip, he continued to be the heart and soul of the celebration each year. But more than that, he had awakened a sense of joy and creativity in his fellow penguins that lasted all year round.

And so, in the land of eternal Christmas Day sun, a unique tradition was born. It just went to show that the spirit of Christmas could thrive anywhere - even in the coldest, most remote corner of the world.

So, little ones, remember Pip and his penguin parade. It teaches us that Christmas spirit isn't about where you are or what you have. It's about coming together, being creative, and spreading joy in your own unique way. Whether you're in a snowy town or on an icy Antarctic shore, the magic of Christmas can always find a way to shine through.

Chapter 23:
The Runaway Wreath

In a quaint little town called Evergreen, where Christmas spirit hung in the air like the scent of freshly baked cookies, there lived a very special wreath. This wreath, you see, was no ordinary circle of pine boughs and holly. It was magical, though nobody knew it yet.

The wreath had been lovingly crafted by old Mrs. Winters, whose tiny shop on Main Street was famous for its beautiful Christmas decorations. She had woven it from the most fragrant evergreen branches, adorned it with pinecones and red berries, and finished it with a perfectly tied velvet bow. But as she worked, Mrs. Winters had hummed an ancient Christmas melody, one that her grandmother had taught her long ago. Little did she know, this song had awakened something special in the wreath.

On a crisp December morning, the wreath was purchased by Mayor Hawthorne, who planned to hang it on the grand doors of Town Hall. As he carried it down Main Street, the wreath began to feel a strange sensation. It wanted to move!

Suddenly, a gust of wind caught the wreath, lifting it right out of the Mayor's hands. "Oh my!" exclaimed Mayor Hawthorne, watching in disbelief as the wreath rolled down the street like a festive hoop.

The wreath bounced and rolled, reveling in its newfound freedom. It had spent its entire existence hanging still, and now it wanted to explore! As it rolled along, it left a trail of Christmas cheer in its wake.

First, it passed by the local bakery. The baker, Mr. Gruber, was struggling to come up with a design for his annual Christmas cake competition. As the wreath rolled by, shedding a few pine needles and berries, Mr. Gruber's eyes lit up with inspiration. "That's it!" he exclaimed, quickly sketching a wreath-shaped cake design.

Next, the wreath bounced past Miss Libby's first-grade class, who were on a winter walk. The children squealed with delight at the sight of the rolling decoration. Miss Libby, seizing the teachable moment, turned it into a fun lesson about circles and motion. The wreath had just made science class a lot more festive!

As it continued its journey, the wreath rolled through the park where the high school choir was practicing for their Christmas concert. They had been struggling with their rendition of "Deck the Halls," but something about the sight of the rolling wreath sparked their enthusiasm. Suddenly, their "fa la la la las" were pitch-perfect and full of Christmas spirit.

The wreath's adventure continued throughout the day. It rolled past the fire station, where the firefighters were decorating their truck for the Christmas parade. Inspired by the runaway wreath, they decided to create a "rolling wreath" float, complete with twinkling lights.

At the animal shelter, the wreath's passing inspired the volunteers to make miniature wreaths to adorn the cages, making them more festive and appealing to potential adopters.

It even made its way to the outskirts of town, where old Mr. Thompson lived alone in his farmhouse. Mr. Thompson hadn't celebrated Christmas since his wife passed away years ago, but the sight of the cheerful wreath rolling past his window stirred something in his heart. For the first time in years, he felt a flicker of Christmas spirit.

As evening fell, the wreath found itself rolling back into town. By now, all of Evergreen was buzzing with talk of the mysterious rolling wreath. Some called it a Christmas miracle, others a festive phenomenon. But everyone agreed that the town hadn't felt this much Christmas cheer in years.

Finally, the wreath rolled to a stop right in the town square, coming to rest at the base of the giant Christmas tree. As if on cue, the tree's lights flickered to life, bathing the wreath in a warm, colorful glow.

A crowd had gathered, drawn by the commotion. Mayor Hawthorne pushed his way to the front, his eyes wide with amazement as he recognized his runaway purchase.

"Well, I'll be," he chuckled, gently picking up the wreath. "You've certainly led us on a merry chase!"

That's when Mrs. Winters stepped forward, her eyes twinkling. "You know," she said softly, "my grandmother used to tell me stories about magical Christmas decorations that would spread joy throughout a town. I always thought they were just fairy tales, but now..." she trailed off, looking at the wreath with wonder.

The Mayor looked around at the gathered townspeople, noticing the smiles on their faces and the sparkle in their eyes. He made a decision right then and there.

"Friends," he announced, holding up the wreath, "I bought this wreath to hang on the Town Hall doors. But I think it's clear that this special wreath belongs to all of Evergreen. What do you say we give it a place of honor right here on our town Christmas tree?"

The crowd cheered their approval. With great ceremony, the Mayor hung the wreath on a sturdy branch right in the middle of the tree, where everyone could see it.

From that moment on, the wreath's magic seemed to spread throughout Evergreen. The town had always celebrated Christmas, but now there was an extra sparkle in the decorations, an added warmth in people's smiles, and a deeper meaning in their "Merry Christmas" greetings.

Mr. Gruber won the cake competition with his wreath-inspired design. The school Christmas pageant, featuring Miss Libby's class rolling across the stage like little wreaths, was a huge hit. The high school choir's performance brought tears to everyone's eyes with its beauty.

The fire department's "rolling wreath" float won first prize in the Christmas parade. The animal shelter saw a record number of adoptions, with families charmed by the festive miniature wreaths. And old Mr. Thompson, inspired by the wreath's journey, invited the entire town to a Christmas Eve party at his farm - the first time he'd opened his doors in years.

As for the wreath itself, it seemed content in its new home on the town Christmas tree. But those who looked closely swore they could sometimes see it quiver, as if it might take off on another adventure at any moment.

From that year on, the story of the runaway wreath became a cherished part of Evergreen's Christmas lore. Parents would tell their children about the magical wreath that rolled through town, spreading Christmas cheer wherever it went. And every year, as the town gathered to light the Christmas tree, they would cheer extra loudly when the lights illuminated their special wreath.

Mrs. Winters, with a knowing smile, began teaching the ancient Christmas melody to anyone who wanted to learn. "You never know," she'd say with a wink, "what kind of magic a simple song might awaken."

And so, in the little town of Evergreen, Christmas was forever changed by a wreath that decided to roll away. It showed everyone that sometimes, the best way to spread Christmas cheer is to break free from where you're hung and roll right into people's hearts.

So, little ones, remember the tale of the runaway wreath. It teaches us that Christmas magic can appear in the most unexpected ways, and that sometimes, a little bit of whimsy and adventure is all it takes to awaken the Christmas spirit in everyone's heart. Who knows? Maybe the decorations in your house have a little magic of their own, just waiting to spread joy in their own special way.

Chapter 24:
The Time Santa Overslept

'Twas the night before Christmas, and all through the North Pole, not a creature was stirring, save for a few busy elves. The workshop was quiet, the sleigh was all packed, and Santa Claus himself was nestled snug in his bed.

But something was amiss on this Christmas Eve. You see, in all the excitement of the holiday preparations, someone had forgotten to set Santa's alarm clock.

As the hours ticked by and the world waited in anticipation, Santa Claus slept on, blissfully unaware that he was about to be very, very late.

It was Jingle, the youngest elf in Santa's workshop, who first noticed something was wrong. As the big clock in the town square struck midnight, Jingle realized that Santa's sleigh was still parked outside the workshop.

"Oh no!" Jingle gasped, his pointy ears quivering with worry. "Santa should have left hours ago!"

Jingle raced through the elf village, his little bells jingling in alarm. He burst into the workshop, where a few elves were putting the finishing touches on some last-minute toys.

"Wake up, everyone!" Jingle cried. "Santa's overslept!"

The news spread like wildfire through the North Pole. Elves tumbled out of bed, still in their striped pajamas. Reindeer pranced nervously in their stables. Even the snowmen stood at attention, their coal eyes wide with concern.

A crowd gathered outside Santa's cozy house, but no one dared to go in and wake him. Santa Claus was known for his jolly demeanor, but he could be a bit grumpy if his sleep was interrupted.

"What are we going to do?" fretted Holly, the head toy maker. "If Santa doesn't wake up soon, he'll never deliver all the presents in time!"

"Christmas will be ruined!" wailed Pepper, the candy cane decorator.

Amidst the panic, Mrs. Claus appeared on the front porch, still in her dressing gown. "Now, now," she said, her voice calm and reassuring. "Let's not lose our heads. We can figure this out together."

The elves huddled around Mrs. Claus, their pointed hats bobbing as they nodded in agreement.

"First things first," Mrs. Claus said. "We need to wake Santa. Any volunteers?"

The crowd fell silent. Waking Santa was a daunting task indeed.

Finally, little Jingle stepped forward. "I'll do it, Mrs. Claus," he said, his voice shaking only slightly.

Mrs. Claus smiled warmly. "Thank you, Jingle. You're very brave. Now, here's what you need to do..."

Jingle listened carefully to Mrs. Claus's instructions, then tiptoed into the house. The only sound was Santa's gentle snoring, which seemed to shake the very foundations of the building.

In the bedroom, Jingle found Santa fast asleep, his red hat askew and his beard tangled. Taking a deep breath, Jingle began to carry out Mrs. Claus's plan.

First, he wafted the scent of freshly baked cookies under Santa's nose. Santa's nostrils twitched, but he slept on.

Next, Jingle jingled his bells right next to Santa's ear. Santa mumbled something about "merry Christmas to all," but didn't wake.

Finally, Jingle brought out the big guns. He leaned close to Santa's ear and whispered, "Santa, I think I just saw a child on the Naughty List do something nice!"

Santa's eyes flew open. "What? Who? Where?" he sputtered, sitting up so quickly that his hat fell off entirely.

As Santa blinked in confusion, Jingle explained the situation. Santa's eyes grew wide with dismay.

"Oh my goodness!" Santa exclaimed, leaping out of bed. "We must hurry!"

Santa rushed to get dressed, somehow managing to get tangled in his own beard in the process. Mrs. Claus hurried in to help, smoothing his beard and straightening his hat.

"Now, don't you worry," Mrs. Claus said soothingly. "The elves and I have a plan."

Outside, the North Pole was a flurry of activity. Elves were triple-checking the naughty and nice lists, reindeer were doing last-minute flight exercises, and Mrs. Claus's helpers were preparing a special batch of turbo-charged cocoa to help Santa stay awake.

As Santa emerged from the house, the crowd cheered. But there was no time for celebrations. They had a lot of work to do and very little time to do it.

"Alright, everyone," Santa called out, his voice booming across the North Pole. "We've got a Christmas to save!"

The plan was ambitious. Instead of Santa visiting each house one by one, the elves would be divided into teams, each led by a reindeer. They would help Santa deliver presents simultaneously across different parts of the world.

Rudolph, with his shiny nose, would guide Santa's sleigh as usual. But now, Dasher, Dancer, Prancer, and the rest would each lead a team of elves in miniature sleighs, all loaded with presents.

"Remember," Santa instructed, "be quick, be quiet, and most importantly, be filled with Christmas spirit. That's what gives us our magic!"

With a flourish of his hand, Santa used his Christmas magic to shrink all the presents to a manageable size for the elves. He then touched each elf gently on the head, granting them the ability to slide down chimneys for one night only.

As the teams prepared to take off, Jingle approached Santa nervously. "Um, Santa?" he said. "What about me? Do I have a team?"

Santa knelt down beside the little elf, his eyes twinkling. "Jingle, my boy, you have the most important job of all. You're coming with me. After all, I might need someone to wake me up if I doze off again!"

Jingle's face lit up with joy. He scrambled into Santa's sleigh, settling himself right next to the big red bag of toys.

With a crack of the reins and a mighty "Ho ho ho!", Santa's sleigh took off into the night sky. Behind him, eight other sleighs followed, each pulled by a reindeer and filled with eager elves.

The night that followed was one that would go down in Christmas history. Across the world, children who stayed up late to catch a glimpse of Santa were amazed to see not one, but multiple magical sleighs soaring across the sky.

In New York, a team led by Dasher expertly navigated the skyscrapers. In Tokyo, Dancer's team delighted in the neon lights as they zipped from house to house. Prancer's team had a close call with a kangaroo in Australia but managed to deliver all their presents without a hitch.

Meanwhile, Santa, with Jingle by his side, focused on the most remote areas and the children who needed a little extra Christmas magic. More than once, Jingle had to jingle his bells loudly to keep Santa from nodding off, but together they made sure no child was forgotten.

As the first light of dawn began to color the eastern sky, the sleighs all converged back at the North Pole. Tired but happy elves tumbled out, chattering excitedly about their adventures.

Santa stepped out of his sleigh, stretched his back, and surveyed his helpers with pride. "Well done, everyone!" he boomed. "Thanks to your quick thinking and teamwork, we've managed to save Christmas!"

A cheer went up from the crowd. Even the reindeer joined in, their joyful brays echoing across the snowy landscape.

As the excitement died down, Santa turned to Jingle. "And thank you, Jingle," he said warmly. "If you hadn't raised the alarm and been brave enough to wake me, none of this would have been possible."

Jingle blushed to the tips of his pointy ears. "I was just doing my job, Santa," he mumbled shyly.

"Indeed you were," Santa chuckled. "And you've given me a wonderful idea. From now on, you shall be my official alarm clock elf. It'll be your job to make sure I'm always up in time for Christmas Eve."

Jingle's eyes widened with delight. It was the highest honor an elf could receive.

As the North Pole settled down for a well-deserved rest, Santa gathered everyone for one last announcement.

"My friends," he said, "we've learned an important lesson today. Christmas isn't about one person doing everything perfectly. It's about coming together, helping each other, and spreading joy however we can. From now on, let's remember that every day, not just when we oversleep!"

Everyone laughed and agreed. And so, a potential Christmas disaster had turned into one of the most memorable and meaningful holidays ever.

In the years that followed, the story of the time Santa overslept became a favorite tale at the North Pole. It reminded everyone that with a little creativity, a lot of teamwork, and a dash of Christmas magic, any challenge could be overcome.

And Jingle? Well, he took his new responsibility very seriously. Every Christmas Eve, right on time, the North Pole would ring with the sound of his bells, ensuring that Santa Claus was always ready to bring Christmas joy to children around the world.

So, little ones, if you ever worry about Santa being late on Christmas Eve, just listen carefully. You might hear the faint jingling of bells, carried on the winter wind – a sign that Jingle the elf is making sure Christmas will arrive right on time.

Chapter 25:
The North Pole Talent Show

In the magical realm of the North Pole, where the Northern Lights dance across the sky and the snow sparkles like diamond dust, there was a buzz of excitement in the air. It was time for the annual North Pole Talent Show, a spectacular event where elves, reindeer, and even Santa himself showcased their special abilities.

This year was particularly special because it marked the 1000th anniversary of the talent show. Santa had announced that the winner would receive a truly magnificent prize: their act would be incorporated into the Christmas Eve journey, becoming a new holiday tradition for children around the world.

As news of the grand prize spread, everyone at the North Pole was aflutter with anticipation. Elves who had never considered themselves particularly talented were suddenly practicing juggling acts with ornaments. Reindeer were choreographing elaborate flying routines. Even the snowmen were trying to perfect their best magic tricks (which mostly involved pulling carrots out of their snowy hats).

Among all the excitement was Holly, a young elf with bright green eyes and a mop of curly red hair that always escaped from under her pointed hat. Holly had a secret talent that she'd never shared with anyone – she could communicate with Christmas trees. It had started as a whisper, a faint rustling of needles that slowly formed into words. Over time, Holly had learned to understand and speak back to the trees.

As the talent show approached, Holly debated whether she should enter. Would anyone believe her talent was real? And even if they did, how could talking to Christmas trees possibly help on the Christmas Eve journey?

It was Twinkle, Holly's best friend, who finally convinced her to sign up. "Holly," Twinkle said, her eyes sparkling with excitement, "your talent is amazing! And who knows? Maybe understanding Christmas trees could be more useful than you think!"

So, with butterflies in her stomach, Holly added her name to the sign-up sheet.

The day of the talent show arrived, and the North Pole's grand auditorium was packed. Santa and Mrs. Claus sat in the front row, beaming with pride at their talented North Pole family.

The show began with a bang – literally. The Firecracker Elves put on a dazzling display of safe, indoor fireworks that spelled out "Merry Christmas" in the air. Next came the Reindeer Synchronized Flying Team, led by Dasher, who performed loop-de-loops and figure eights that left the audience gasping in awe.

Act after act took the stage, each more impressive than the last. There was Frosty the Snowman, who had learned to play "Jingle Bells" by clacking his coal buttons. The Cookie Elves performed a delicious ballet, pirouetting across the stage in costumes made entirely of gingerbread. Even Rudolph got into the act, using his shiny red nose to create a spectacular light show.

As Holly waited backstage for her turn, her nervousness grew. How could she compete with all these amazing acts? She was seriously considering sneaking out the back door when she heard her name announced.

Taking a deep breath, Holly walked onto the stage. The audience fell silent, curious about what this little elf's talent might be.

"Um, hello everyone," Holly began, her voice shaky. "My talent is... well, I can talk to Christmas trees."

There was a moment of confused silence, then a ripple of gentle laughter spread through the audience. They thought she was joking!

Determined to prove herself, Holly turned to the giant Christmas tree that stood at the side of the stage. "Excuse me," she said politely. "Would you mind saying hello to everyone?"

To the astonishment of all, the tree's branches began to sway, and a deep, rumbling voice filled the auditorium. "Hello, North Pole friends! Merry Christmas!"

Gasps of surprise echoed through the room. Santa leaned forward in his seat, his eyes twinkling with interest.

Encouraged, Holly continued her conversation with the tree. She asked about its journey from the forest, and the tree regaled the audience with tales of the woodland creatures it had known. Holly translated as the tree shared ancient Christmas legends passed down through generations of evergreens.

As Holly's act came to a close, the auditorium erupted in applause. Even the other contestants were cheering, amazed by this unique and magical talent.

The judges huddled together, whispering excitedly. After what seemed like an eternity, Santa stood up to announce the winner.

"My friends," he said, his voice filled with joy, "in all my centuries, I've never seen anything quite like this. Holly, your talent is not only extraordinary, but it opens up a whole new world of Christmas magic for us to explore. You are the winner of this year's North Pole Talent Show!"

Holly could hardly believe her pointy ears. She had won!

As the crowd cheered, Santa explained how Holly's talent would become part of the Christmas Eve journey. "From now on," he declared, "Holly will communicate with the Christmas trees in each home we visit. The trees will tell us about the children who live there – their hopes, their dreams, and their Christmas wishes. This will help us bring even more joy and wonder to every child on Christmas morning!"

In the days that followed, preparations began for incorporating Holly's talent into the Christmas Eve routine. She worked with the elves in the workshop, helping them understand the secret wishes that children whispered to their Christmas trees. She aided the reindeer, using the trees' knowledge to plan the most efficient route around the world.

As Christmas Eve approached, excitement at the North Pole reached fever pitch. Everyone was eager to see how Holly's unique ability would enhance the magic of the night.

When the big night finally arrived, Holly took her place in Santa's sleigh, right next to the big red bag of toys. As they soared through the sky, Holly felt a thrill of anticipation.

At the first house, Holly listened carefully to the Christmas tree in the living room. "Santa," she whispered, "the little boy who lives here is worried that you won't come because he accidentally broke an ornament last week. The tree says he's been extra good ever since, trying to make up for it."

Santa's eyes twinkled. "Well then, we'll just have to leave him an extra special gift to show him he's still on the Nice List!"

And so it went, all through the night. At each home, Holly's conversations with the Christmas trees provided valuable insights, allowing Santa to tailor his visits to each child's needs and wishes.

There was the little girl whose tree told Holly about her secret dream of becoming an astronaut, prompting Santa to leave a telescope among her gifts. And the twins who had been quarreling all month – their tree suggested leaving them gifts that would encourage them to play together.

As the night wore on, it became clear that Holly's talent was indeed making this Christmas more magical than ever before. The Christmas trees, overjoyed at finally being able to share their knowledge, went above and beyond in their help. Some even reshaped their branches to make it easier for Santa to access difficult chimneys!

By the time they returned to the North Pole, as the first light of Christmas dawn was breaking, everyone agreed that this had been the most successful Christmas Eve journey yet.

At the North Pole's Christmas morning celebration, Santa raised a toast to Holly. "My dear," he said warmly, "your special talent has brought a new level of magic and understanding to our Christmas mission. From this day forward, you shall be known as Holly the Christmas Tree Whisperer, a vital part of our Christmas team!"

Holly beamed with pride, her heart full of joy. She had found her place in the Christmas magic, and she knew that every Christmas from now on would be filled with the whispers of trees and the deepest wishes of children's hearts.

As the celebrations continued, with elves dancing and reindeer prancing, Holly took a moment to thank the giant Christmas tree that had helped her reveal her talent at the show.

"Thank you," she said softly. "You've helped make this the best Christmas ever."

The tree's branches rustled gently. "No, Holly," it replied. "Thank you for helping all of us Christmas trees fulfill our greatest wish – to be a true part of the Christmas magic. Merry Christmas, little elf."

"Merry Christmas," Holly whispered back, her heart full of the true spirit of the season.

And so, dear children, as you gather around your own Christmas tree this year, remember Holly's story. Perhaps, if you listen very carefully, you might hear your tree whispering too. For now we know that Christmas trees are more than just beautiful decorations – they are the silent guardians of our Christmas wishes, helping Santa bring magic and joy to every home.

Conclusion:
The Magic of Christmas Stories

Dear Reader,

As we come to the end of our journey through these Christmas tales, we hope the magic of the season has found its way into your heart. From The Littlest Reindeer to The North Pole Talent Show, each story has been a window into the wonder and joy that make Christmas so special.

We've traveled to the North Pole and back, met elves and reindeer, talking snowmen and magical wreaths. We've seen how the smallest acts of kindness can make the biggest difference, and how the true spirit of Christmas can be found in the most unexpected places.

Remember Tinsel's curiosity that bridged two worlds, Pip the penguin's determination to bring Christmas joy to Antarctica, and Holly's unique gift of talking to Christmas trees. These characters, and all the others you've met in these pages, remind us that everyone has something special to contribute to the magic of Christmas.

As you close this book, we hope you'll carry these stories with you throughout the year. Maybe you'll listen a little more closely to the whispers of your Christmas tree, or look out for runaway wreaths spreading joy in your neighborhood. Perhaps you'll find yourself inspired to create your own Christmas magic, just like our storybook friends.

Remember, the spirit of Christmas isn't confined to these pages or even to one day of the year. It lives in every act of kindness, every moment of wonder, and every heart that believes in the magic of the season.

So, from all of us at the North Pole - Santa, Mrs. Claus, the elves, the reindeer, and even the talking snowmen - we wish you a very Merry

Christmas and a year filled with joy, love, and a little bit of magic.

Until next Christmas, keep believing!